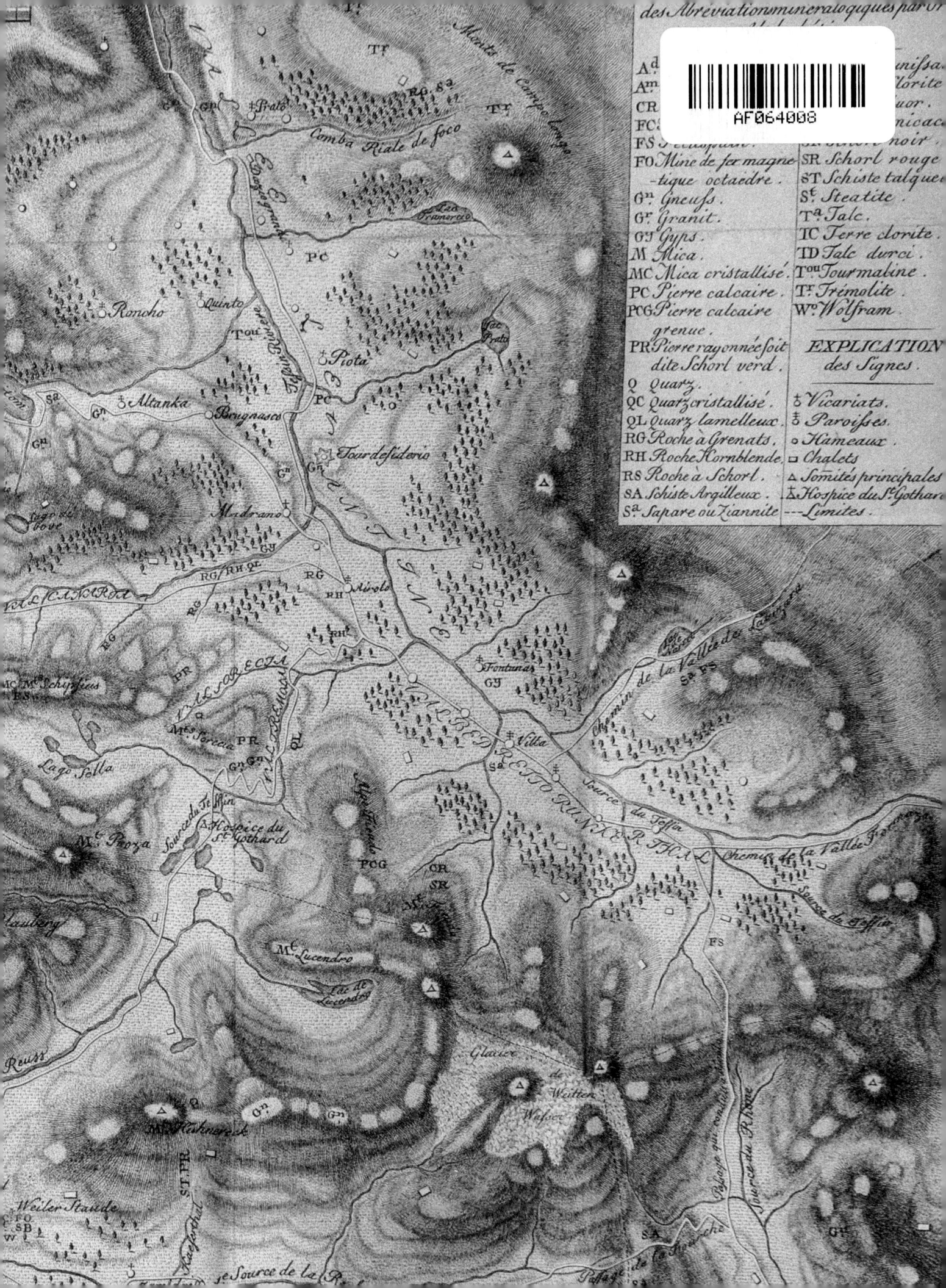

STEFAN BOGNER • JAN KARL BAEDEKER

PORSCHE DRIVE – PASS PORTRAIT

GOTTHARD

SCHWEIZ – SWITZERLAND – 2108 M

DELIUS KLASING VERLAG

EDITORIAL

Meine persönliche Gotthardgeschichte beginnt mit einem verschwommenen Erinnerungsbild aus meiner Kindheit. Ich sitze im Fond unseres alten Käfers, blättere in einem Micky-Maus-Heft, schiebe immer wieder die Frottee-Handtücher zur Seite, die wir zum Schutz vor der Sonne in die Fenster geklemmt haben, und bestaune die gewaltigen Felswände, die rechts und links in den Himmel ragen. Hinten im Heck dröhnt und brummte der bescheidene Boxermotor nach Leibeskräften, damit wir von der steilen Höh nicht in die nächste Schlucht hinabrutschten – so zumindest male ich es mir aus.

Für mich war es deshalb nur schlüssig, dass der Gotthard auch so hieß, wie er auf mich wirkte – nämlich groß, hart, allmächtig. Der Gotthardpass war die Schwelle, die es auf dem Weg ans Mittelmeer zu passieren galt, die letzte Hürde vor dieser schier endlosen, nach Sand, Sonnencreme und Salzwasser duftenden Zeit der großen Ferien. Oben an der Passhöhe angelangt, schien es mir dann, als könne man am Horizont im Dunst schon die Segelboote erspähen, die auf den Wellen des Mittelmeers tanzten. In keinem Moment brannte das Gefühl der Vorfreude und des Fernwehs so stark wie hier oben in der kalten Bergluft am Pass, 2.108 Meter über dem Meer und nur noch wenige Autostunden von der Küste entfernt. Und wenn es nach Wochen unter der brennenden Mittelmeersonne wieder nach Norden ging und sich über dem Gotthard der Himmel grau verfinsterte, erfüll-

My personal Gotthard story begins with a hazy memory from my childhood. I'm sitting in the rear of our old Beetle, leafing through a Mickey Mouse comic book. I keep pushing the terry towelling cloths that we've stuck to the window for sun protection aside to gaze at the huge rock faces that tower into the sky on the right and the left. At the rear of the car, a modest boxer engine whines and groans with might and main so that we don't slide from the lofty heights and plummet into the gorge below – at least that's how I see it.

So, for me, it was only logical that the Gotthard name should also fit the impression it made on me: namely big, tough, almighty. The Gotthard Pass was the threshold that had to be crossed on the way to the Mediterranean, the last hurdle before the seemingly endless, sand-sun-and-saltwater-scented time of the long summer holidays. Arriving at the top of the pass, it seemed to me as though you could already see the haze on the horizon, and the sailboats that danced on the waves of the Mediterranean. At no other time did the feeling of excited wanderlust burn as strongly as it did up there in the cold mountain air of the pass, at 2,108 metres above sea level yet only a few hours by car from the coast. And when it was time to head north again after weeks under the hot Mediterranean sun, up over the Gotthard where the sky was dark grey, into

ten mich die saftig-grünen Matten des Urserentals, die gewaltigen Wasserfälle und die dramatisch-dunklen Felsen am Südufer des Vierwaldstättersees mit jener glühenden Euphorie der Heimkehr, die man wohl nur als Kind in dieser Intensität erfährt.

Wahrscheinlich stammt dieses Erinnerungsbild nicht einmal von einer einzigen Fahrt – vermutlich setzt es sich vielmehr aus all den Reisen über den Gotthard zusammen, die ich in meiner Kindheit und Jugend erlebt habe. Irgendwann fuhren wir nicht mehr über den Pass, sondern nahmen den Tunnel, wo man die Comics mit der Taschenlampe lesen musste und keine Segelboote mehr in der Ferne flimmern sah. Und doch blieb der Gotthard für mich ein starkes Symbol des Übergangs und der Erwartung. So persönlich mir diese Eindrücke und Erinnerungen immer erschienen, so exemplarisch sind sie doch – zu dieser Erkenntnis gelangte ich zumindest während der Arbeit an diesem Buch – für die Bilder und Gefühle, die der Gotthard in der kollektiven Erinnerung über Jahrhunderte und Generationen hinweg mit veränderten Vorzeichen hinterlassen hat. Ob es nun die ersten Saumhändler waren, die den beschwerlichen Weg über den Pass mit ihren Mauseln auf sich nahmen, um in den Tälern jenseits des großen Berges Milch und Käse zu verkaufen. Oder die Bildungsreisenden der Romantik, die in den Postkuschen über den Pass zu den Ruinen Italiens schaukelten. Immer waren die Reisenden erfüllt von einer ganz eigenen Sehnsucht nach dem, was sie auf der anderen Seite erwartete. Stets war der Gotthard ein Ort der Passage, an dem man nicht nur die Alpen überquerte, sondern auch selbst auf die eine oder andere Art transformiert wurde. Um das Jahr 1200, als der Gotthardpass durch die ersten Brückenbauten in der wilden Schöllenenschlucht für den Handelsverkehr erschlossen wurde, brauchte man noch viel Mut und Zeit, um aus dem Urnerland im Norden in die südliche Leventina zu wandern. Doch mit stetigem Ausbau des Saumweges, den ersten Alpentunnels, der für Kutschen befahrbaren Poststraße aus dem Jahr 1830, der spektakulären, 1882 in Betrieb genommenen Gotthardeisenbahn und dem 1980 eröffneten Straßentunnel durchs Gotthardmassiv wurden die Zeit und Energie, die man für die Überwindung der Zentralalpen aufbringen musste, immer geringer. Heute dauert die Bahnfahrt durch den Basistunnel – mit 57 Kilometern immerhin der längste Eisenbahntunnel der Welt – keine 20 Minuten mehr. Wer spätabends nach einem Wochenend-Trip mit dem Zug von Mailand nach Zürich zurückfährt und auf sein Smartphone starrt, wird den Gotthard wahrscheinlich kaum noch bemerken.

Doch das Streben nach Komfort und Beschleunigung hat seinen Preis: Wenn der Weg sich bis zum Extrem verkürzt und verschlankt, kann er kein Ziel mehr sein. Und man muss wahrlich kein Glücksforscher oder Drehbuchautor aus Hollywood sein, um zu verstehen, dass man als Mensch mitunter gewisse Herausforderungen und Strapazen durchleben muss, um wiederum mit großen

the lush green meadows of the Ursern Valley and past the mighty waterfalls and the dramatic dark rocks along the southern shore of Lake Lucerne, I was filled with that glowing euphoria of coming home, a feeling that probably only children can experience with such intensity.

This recollection is very likely not from one trip but rather a collage of memories from the many trips I undertook over the Gotthard during my childhood and teenage years. At some point we stopped driving over the pass, opting instead for the tunnel route, where we had to read our comic books with a torch light and no longer spotted sailboats glimmering on the horizon. Yet, the Gotthard remained imprinted in my mind as a symbol of transition and anticipation. As personal as these impressions and recollections seemed to me, they are in fact illustrative of the images and feelings that the Gotthard has left in the collective memories garnered over centuries and generations throughout the ages. At least this is what I learned while working on this book. Whether it was the first muleteers who made the arduous journey over the pass with their pack animals to sell milk and cheese to the valley dwellers on the other side of the great mountain, or the knowledge-seeking travellers of the Romantic era, whose bones got shaken in the post coaches over the pass on their way to the ruins of Italy. In any case, all of these wayfarers were filled with a yearning to discover what awaited them on the other side. The Gotthard was always a 'rite of passage' where one not only crossed the Alps, but also underwent a transformation in one way or the other.

Around the year 1200, when the Gotthard Pass was opened up for commercial trade with the first bridges of the wild Schöllenen Gorge, travellers still needed courage and time to hike from the canton of Uri in the north to the Leventina in the south. However, with the ongoing expansion of the bridle paths, the first Alpine tunnels, which made the post road passable for the stagecoaches in 1830, the spectacular Gotthard Railway which went into operation in 1882, and the Gotthard road tunnel which opened a route through the massif in 1980, the time and energy needed to traverse the Central Alps became increasingly less. Today, the train ride through the base tunnel – still the world's longest railway tunnel at 57-kilometres long – takes less than 20 minutes. If you travel by train from Milan to Zurich after a weekend sojourn and have eyes only for your Smartphone, you'll probably miss the entire Gotthard passage.

Nevertheless, the pursuit of comfort and speed has its price: if the path is radically shortened and streamlined, it can no longer be considered a destination. And one doesn't necessarily have to be a happiness researcher or Hollywood scriptwriter to understand that, to be

Emotionen belohnt zu werden. Und dass es sich gerade an Durchgangsorten lohnen kann, einmal aus dem Verkehrsfluss auszuscheren, den Motor abzustellen und sich genauer umzusehen.

In den letzten Jahren sind Stefan Bogner und ich immer wieder zum Gotthard gereist. Wir haben viel Zeit in den Bergen des Massivs verbracht – der Gotthard ist schließlich kein einzelner Gipfel, sondern eine ganze Gebirgsgruppe – und die Kurven der Straße mit dem Auto, dem Helikopter, zu Fuß erkundet. Wir haben auf der Passhöhe übernachtet, Schneestürmen und Gewittern getrotzt, in den Gasthäusern die lokalen Spezialitäten gekostet. Wir haben in Archiven alte Straßenkarten studiert und uns durch viele Jahrhunderte Verkehrsgeschichte gelesen. Wir sind bei Nebel in den Steilhängen herumgeklettert, um das perfekte Bild einzufangen, und morgens allein über die Tremola in den Sonnenaufgang gebraust, während sich unten vor dem Tunnelportal bereits die Reisebusse stauten. So haben wir eine einzigartige Kulturlandschaft kennen und schätzen gelernt, die für uns selbst zum Ziel unserer Reiselust geworden ist.

Der Gotthard mag die Alpenverbindung der Superlative sein. Als Quelle und Wasserscheide Europas, Wiege und Festung der Schweiz, Schauplatz von Feldzügen, geopolitisches Zünglein an der Waage des kontinentalen Machtgefüges, Nadelöhr und Hochdruckbeschleuniger des Waren- und Personenverkehrs zwischen Nord und Süd hat er in den Geschichtsbüchern so viele Spuren hinterlassen wie kein anderer Alpenübergang. Und doch verblasst die historische Relevanz hinter dem ganz persönlichen Gotthard-Erlebnis, das sich jedem Passreisenden bietet, der dem uralten Saumpfad, den mittelalterlichen Brücken, dem Natursteinpflasterkehren der Kunststraße und den brutalistischen Beton-Viadukten der Nachkriegszeit folgt und seine Sinne öffnet für die Kontraste der Architektur, Topografie und Landschaft, die Wechsel des Klimas und der Kulturen. Der Gotthard ist vor allem ein Gefühl – so kommt es, dass zwischen den tosenden Wildwassern der Reuss und den ehrwürdigen Kurven der Tremola man nicht nur die Zeugnisse einer einmaligen Passgeschichte findet, sondern mit etwas Glück auch zu sich selbst.

rewarded with great emotion, humans must sometimes go through certain challenges and hardships. And it may just be worth the effort at the transit points to turn off the ignition and take a closer look around.

In recent years, Stefan Bogner and I have returned time and again to the Gotthard. We've spent a lot of time in the mountains of this massif – after all, the Gotthard is not a single peak, but a whole mountain range – exploring the curves of the road with the car, a helicopter and on foot. We've stayed overnight at the pass, we've defied blizzards and thunderstorms, we've tasted local specialties at guest houses and inns. We've pored over old road maps in archives and read through many centuries of traffic history. We've clambered around the steep cliffs in fog to capture the perfect image, and raced over the Tremola in the early morning at sunrise, while far below at the tunnel portal, the travel buses queue. This is how we have come to know and appreciate a very special cultural landscape that has, in itself, become the destination of our wanderlust.

The Gotthard may well be the transalpine route of superlatives. As a source and watershed of Europe, the cradle and fortress of Switzerland, the stage for military campaigns, the geopolitical tipping of balance of continental power structure, the bottleneck and high-pressure accelerator of goods and passenger transport between the north and south – it has left more traces in the history books than any other Alpine crossing. And yet the historic relevance fades behind the very personal Gotthard experience that is offered to every pass traveller who follows the medieval bridges, the natural stone-paved switchbacks and the brutal concrete viaducts of the postwar era, and whose senses are open to the contrast of architecture, topography and landscape, the changing of climate and cultures. More than anything, the Gotthard is a feeling, and it can happen that between the roaring rapids of the Reuss and the time-honoured curves of the Tremola, one not only discovers evidence of an unparalleled pass history, but also, with a little luck, finds a way back to oneself.

STEFAN BOGNER ist Autor, Fotograf und Inhaber einer Designagentur – und ein leidenschaftlicher Porsche-Fahrer. Mit seinen eindrücklichen Fotografien von Kurven, Kehren und Serpentinen hat er die Schönheit der Alpenpässe sichtbar gemacht. Sein Magazin *Curves* und sein Bildband *Escapes* gelten unter sportlichen Automobilisten als perfekte Anleitungen zum Glücklichsein.

Stefan Bogner is a writer, photographer, founder of a Munich Design Agency – and a passionate Porsche driver. With his stunning photos of curves, hairpins and serpentines, he has captured the magnificence of the Alpine passes. Sporty drivers consider his magazine *Curves* and his coffee-table book *Escapes* as the ultimate guides to happiness.

JAN KARL BAEDEKER ist Reisender aus Leidenschaft – und zudem Autor, Fotograf sowie Chefredakteur des Magazins *Classic Driver*. Sozusagen genetisch vorbelastet ist er als Urenkel von Karl Baedeker, der ab 1828 das Reisen zu einer Kulturform erhob und mit seinen roten Reisehandbüchern viele Generationen von Fernwehgetriebenen auf die richtige Spur brachte. Jan Karl Baedeker hat Medienwissenschaften und Europäische Ethnologie in Hamburg studiert, lebt heute in Zürich – und ist immer auf dem Sprung zur nächsten Tour.

Jan Karl Baedeker is an avid traveller – as well as author, photographer and editor-in-chief of the magazine *Classic Driver*. One could say he is genetically predisposed: he is, after all, the great-grandson of Karl Baedeker, who from 1828 turned travelling into a form of culture and, with his red travel guides, opened the way for many generations of adventurers to whet their wanderlust. Jan Karl Baedeker learned Media Studies and European Ethnology in Hamburg, he now lives in Zurich – and is always set to take off on his next adventure.

DIE GESCHICHTE DES GOTTHARDPASSES

THE HISTORY OF THE GOTTHARD PASS

MIT FREUNDLICHER GENEHMIGUNG
COURTESY OF:
STAATSARCHIV KANTON URI
ÖLBILD VON RUDOLF KOLLER

Über keinen anderen Alpenpass wurden derart viele Geschichten erzählt, Bücher geschrieben und Lieder gesungen wie über den Gotthard. Er wurde verehrt und verklärt als höchster Berg der Welt, Dach und Quelle Europas, Bollwerk und Völkerstraße, Wiege und Festung der Schweiz. Er stand als reales wie symbolisches Hindernis zwischen Nord und Süd – und wurde zum Sinnbild kultureller Verbindung. Es fällt nicht leicht, den Gotthard von all den epischen, romantischen, poetischen und propagandistischen Schichten zu befreien, die ihn seit Jahrhunderten überlagern und die jedem Autor, der sich an das törichte Unterfangen seiner literarischen Überquerung wagt, schnell den Kopf vernebeln. Man beginnt zu verstehen, warum Johann Wolfgang von Goethe dreimal an der Passhöhe stand – und immer wieder den Rückzug antrat: Der Gotthard weiß zu überwältigen. Dabei kann man die Geschichte des Gotthardpasses auch als eine Folge von günstigen Fügungen, aberwitzigen Zufällen und erstaunlichen Kausalitätsketten erzählen, als ein komplexes Gewebe lokaler Bedingungen und globaler Entwicklungen, dessen Fäden über die Jahrhunderte zu einem Erzählstoff epischer Dichte zusammengezogen wurden.

Zu Recht werden der Gotthardpass und die Tunnel, die das Gebirgsmassiv durchbohren, als Jahrhundertbauten und Wunderwerke menschlicher Imaginationskraft, Innovationsfähigkeit und Beharrlichkeit gefeiert. Der Gotthard war das Nadelöhr zwischen Nachbarn und Talschaf-

No other Alpine pass has had as many stories told, books written and songs sung about it as the Gotthard. It has been revered and glorified as the highest mountain in the world, the roof and heart of Europe, a bastion and people's road, cradle and fortress of Switzerland. The Gotthard stood as a physical and symbolic barrier between the north and south, and grew to become a symbol of cultural connection. It is no easy task to peel away all the epic, romantic, poetic and propagandistic layers that have blanketed the Gotthard for centuries, which quickly cloud the mind of any author foolish enough to embark on a literary crossing. One begins to grasp why Johann Wolfgang von Goethe reached the top of the pass three times, only to retreat on every occasion: the Gotthard knows how to overwhelm. The history of the Gotthard can also be described as a string of lucky breaks, crazy coincidences and astounding chains of causality, as a complex web of local conditions and global developments, the threads of which have been woven into a narrative of epic intensity over the centuries.

The Gotthard Pass and the tunnels that penetrate the massif are celebrated, justifiably, as monumental structures and marvels of the power of human imagination, innovation and sheer perseverance. The Gotthard was the eye of the needle between neighbours and valley dwellers, between countries and cultures. With its opening, the path was clear for everything that people do when a new realm of possibility suddenly appears. They engage

> **Es lohnt sich, den Gotthard zunächst einmal durch die Brille des Geologen zu betrachten. Im Querschnitt zeigt sich das gewaltige Zentralmassiv der Alpen nämlich alles andere als homogen.**

ten, zwischen Ländern und Kulturen. Mit seiner Öffnung wurde der Weg frei für all das, was Menschen nun einmal anstellen, wenn sich plötzlich ein neuer Möglichkeitsraum öffnet: Sie betreiben Austausch und Handel, Expansion und Krieg. Die Gründe dafür, dass ausgerechnet das Gotthardmassiv zu einem kulturgeschichtlich so entscheidenden Hindernis und Durchgangsort wurde, finden sich allerdings in vormenschlicher Zeit. Die tektonischen Kräfte, die Faltung der zentralen Alpengebirge und der ewige erdgeschichtliche Kreislauf von Schichtung und Erosion formten inmitten des Europäischen Kontinents all jene Gipfel und Grate, Täler und Schluchten, entlang derer und durch welche die alpine Besiedelungs- und Verkehrsgeschichte ihren vorgezeichneten Lauf nahm.

Es lohnt sich, den Gotthard zunächst einmal durch die Brille des Geologen zu betrachten. Im Querschnitt zeigt sich das gewaltige Zentralmassiv der Alpen nämlich alles andere als homogen. Vielmehr reihen und reiben sich viele verschiedene Gesteinsschichten mit unterschiedlichsten Eigenschaften und Strukturen aneinander. Zwischen dem Aaremassiv im Norden und dem Gotthardmassiv im Süden, die beide aus harten Gneisen und Graniten bestehen, liegen erdgeschichtlich ältere, tektonisch stark beanspruchte Gebiete wie die Urserenzone und das Tavetscher Zwischenmassiv. Diese sogenannten »Störzonen« bildeten die Grundlage für die topografische Vielfalt des Gotthardübergangs mit seinen sanften Hochtälern und schroffen Schluchten – und stellten die Ingenieure und Tunnelbauer am Gotthard immer wieder vor gewaltige Herausforderungen. Tatsächlich machten sich die Menschen in der Gotthardregion wohl schon vor rund 8.000

> **It is well worthwhile taking a good look at the Gotthard through the eyes of a geologist. A cross-section shows that the mighty range of the Central Alps is anything but homogeneous.**

in exchange and trade, expansion and war. However, the reasons for the Gotthard massif becoming so culturally important historically as a barrier and passageway can be traced back to the time before man roamed the Earth. The tectonic forces, the folding of the Central Alpine chain and the endless geological cycle of stratification and erosion, formed all the peaks and ridges, valleys and gorges in the middle of the European continent, along and through which the story of Alpine colonisation and traffic took its predetermined course.

It is well worthwhile taking a good look at the Gotthard through the eyes of a geologist. A cross-section shows that the mighty range of the Central Alps is anything but homogeneous. On the contrary, many different rock layers with very different characteristics and structures butt and grate against each other. Between the Aarmassif in the north and the Gotthard massif in the south, both made up of hard gneiss and granite, lie geologically older, tectonically heavily stressed areas such as the Ursern Zone and the Tavetsch Massif. These so-called 'fault zones' formed the basis for the topographical diversity of the

MIT FREUNDLICHER GENEHMIGUNG
COURTESY OF:
STAATSARCHIV KANTON URI

Jahren am Berg zu schaffen. In der Urseren – dem Hochtal auf etwa 1.500 Meter Höhe, das zwischen der Schöllenenschlucht im Norden und der Passhöhe des Gotthards im Süden liegt – wurde in der Steinzeit einfacher Bergbau betrieben. Mithilfe von Hirschgeweihen und Feuer löste man Bergkristall aus dem Gestein, etwa an der Stremlücke am Oberalpstock. Steinerne Pfeilspitzen aus der Zeit zwischen 4000 und 2500 v. Chr. erinnern derweil an die Bären, die dem Urserental einmal seinen Namen geben sollten, als auch an die Wölfe, mit denen steinzeitliche Jäger um das Wild konkurrieren mussten. In der Bronze- und Eisenzeit, zwischen 1400 und 450 v. Chr., wurden die Menschen am Gotthard langsam sesshaft. Keramikfunde bei Amsteg deuteten auf eine frühe Siedlung hin. Für internationales Aufsehen sorgten derweil drei keltische Goldringe, die 1962 bei Bauarbeiten in Erstfeld entdeckt und auf die Zeit zwischen 380 und 300 v. Chr. datiert wurden. Heute ist der »Goldschatz von Erstfeld« im Zürcher Landesmuseum zu sehen.

Das Tor in der Schöllenenschlucht

Auch die Römer hinterließen im Urserental ihre Spuren in Form von Münzen. Für Julius Cäsar war der »Adula Mons« – so der römische Name des Gotthards – gar der höchste Berg der Welt. In der Verkehrspolitik des Römischen Reiches spielte der Alpenübergang jedoch keine Rolle. Die Verbindungsstraßen in die Provinzen nördlich der Alpen führten über den Großen Sankt Bernhard, den Septimer, den Splügen, den Simplon, den Reschen, den Brenner. Doch warum wählten die sonst so weitsichtigen römischen Feldherren und Straßenbauer nicht den kürzesten Weg nach Norden? Warum kamen sie zwar regelmäßig über die Gotthard-Passhöhe, machten dann aber im Urserental kehrt – oder traversierten über die Furka, wo sie ein Hospiz betrieben, nach Westen ins Wallis oder über den Oberalppass in die östlich gelegene Provinz Rätien? Für das Römische Imperium waren nur solche Pässe strategisch interessant, über die man im Kriegsfall auch ein ganzes Heer führen konnte. Und obwohl der Weg von Airolo auf die Passhöhe und weiter bis zum heutigen Andermatt trotz aller Gefahren des Hochgebirges vergleichsweise leicht zu erschließen gewesen wäre, stellte die Schöllenenschlucht am nördlichen Ausgang des Urserentals ein nicht zu überwindendes Hindernis dar. Mag sein, dass ein geübter Ziegenhirte über die schroffen, vom Wildwasser der Reuss umtosten Steilhänge kraxeln konnte – für militärische Truppen in voller Montur und Bewaffnung war der direkte Weg hinunter zum Vierwaldstättersee jedoch versperrt.

»Dort am Bätzberg und Teufelsberg bei Urseren an der Matt, da lag das Gotthardproblem«, erkannte der Schweizer Schriftsteller und Literaturnobelpreisträger Carl Spitteler schon 1897 in seinem Buch über den Gotthard. »Dort befand sich das Tor. Allein das Tor war von der Natur geschlossen, und die Natur hatte den Schlüssel nicht danebengelegt.« Tatsächlich sollte das wilde Felsental

Gotthard crossing with its verdant high valleys and rugged ravines, and constantly threw enormous challenges at the engineers and tunnel builders of the Gotthard.

In fact, the people of the Gotthard region were already at work in the mountains around 8,000 years ago. In the Ursern – the high valley at around 1,500 metres altitude between the Schöllenen Gorge in the north and the top of the Gotthard Pass in the south – small-scale mining was practised in the Stone Age. Using deer antlers and fire, the rock crystal was prised from the stones, for example in the Strem Valley on the Oberalpstock. Stone arrowheads from the period spanning 4000 to 2500 BC are a reminder of the bears that apparently gave the Ursern Valley its name, and also the wolves with whom the Stone Age hunters had to compete. In the Bronze and Iron Ages, between 1400 and 450 BC, the people of the Gotthard gradually began to settle. Ceramic remnants at Amsteg give evidence of an early settlement. Three Celtic gold rings, which were discovered in 1962 during construction work in Erstfeld and dated somewhere between 380 and 300 BC, attracted international attention. Today, the 'Gold Treasure of Erstfeld' can be seen in the Zurich State Museum.

The Gate in the Schöllenen Gorge

The Romans also left their traces in the Ursern Valley in the form of coins. For Julius Caesar, the 'Adula Mons', as the Roman's called the Gotthard, was the highest mountain in the world. The Alpine transit route, however, played no role in the Roman Empire's transport policy. The connecting roads in the provinces north of the Alps led over the Great St. Bernard, the Septimer, the Splügen, the Simplon, the Reschen and the Brenner. But why did the otherwise farsighted Roman generals and road builders not choose the shortest way to the north? Why did they regularly take the Gotthard Pass, only to turn back at the Ursern Valley; or traverse the Furka, where they ran a hospice, towards the west into the Valais; or over the Oberalp Pass into the eastern province of Rhaetia? For the Roman Empire, the only passes that were strategically important were the ones over which a whole legion could march in case of war. Although the route from Airolo to the top of the pass and on to today's Andermatt would have been relatively easy to develop despite the perils of the high mountain region, the Schöllenen Gorge at the northern exit of the Ursern Valley posed an insurmountable obstacle. It may well be that a seasoned goat herder could have clambered his way over the craggy, steep-sided escarpment carved out by the raging waters of the Reuss, but for military troops in full gear and armament, the direct route down to the Vierwaldstättersee, now Lake Lucerne, was blocked.

'There at the Bäzberg and Teufelsberg at Ursern on the Matt lay the Gotthard problem,' Carl Spitteler, the Swiss

der Schöllenenschlucht auch nach dem Fall des Römischen Reiches und dem Einsetzen der Völkerwanderungen in Europa noch viele Jahrhunderte lang ein nicht zu überwindendes Hindernis bleiben, das man auf gefährlichen Bergpfaden nur äußerst umständlich und zeitraubend hätte umgehen können. Wer aus dem Tessin direkt nach Norden nach Disentis reisen wollte, wählte den altgedienten Lukmanierpass. Der schnellste Weg ins westlich gelegene Wallis führte über den Simplon. So kam es, dass im Mittelalter auch die deutschen Könige und Kaiser auf ihrem Weg nach Rom anderen Alpenpässen den Vorzug gaben. Von Süden her wurde der Gotthard derweil nur von Tessiner Hirten begangen, die auf den grünen Matten des Hochtals jenseits der Passhöhe ihre Tiere weiden ließen.

Die Gemengelage am Gotthard änderte sich erst im Hochmittelalter. Es ist viel darüber spekuliert worden, was im 12. Jahrhundert – also ein gutes Jahrtausend nach dem Bau der römischen Alpenstraßen – den Ausschlag zur Erschließung der Schöllenen und damit der Erfindung des Gotthardpasses gab. War es jene Revolution der Landwirtschaft um das Jahr 1100, die zur Spezialisierung und Arbeitsteilung unter den Urner Bauern führte, das Prinzip der Alpwirtschaft entstehen ließ – und den lokalen Handels zwischen den vormals isolierten Bergtälern zum Blühen brachte? Hatten der Einzug der Rapperswiler im Urnerland und ein sprunghafter Anstieg der Bevölkerung dafür gesorgt, dass die neuen Talbewohner weiter hinauf in die Berge rückten und nun mit ihren Nachbarn auf den anderen Seiten der Gipfel in Kontakt treten wollten? Waren es religiöse Machthaber wie das Kloster Disentis, dem das Urserental gehörte, oder das Bistum Mailand, das auf der Passhöhe zwischen 1166 und 1176 eine Kapelle geweiht hatte, die nun ihren Einflussbereich vergrößern wollten? Die Gründe werden vielleicht nie restlos aufgedeckt werden. Anders sieht es bei der nicht eben einfachen Frage aus, wer den Pass letztendlich etablierte. Viel spricht inzwischen dafür, dass es die berühmten Walser waren, die auf ihren Wanderungen aus dem Wallis und dem Berner Oberland über die Furka auch ins Urserental übergesiedelt waren und zwischen den Jahren 1190 und 1230 ihre Erfahrungen aus dem hochalpinen Bau von Pfaden und Brücken anwendeten, um die Schöllenen gangbar zu machen. Die Urner Landbesitzer auf der nördlichen Seite der Schlucht dürften ebenfalls dabei geholfen haben, die neuen deutschsprachigen Nachbarn bei ihrem Vorhaben zu unterstützen – und damit nicht nur Zugang zu wichtigen Alpweiden zu erhalten, sondern in der Leventina und Lombardei auch neue Absatzmärkte für ihre Produkte zu erschließen.

Um den Gotthardpass zu öffnen, musste zunächst die Reuss überbrückt werden – und zwar an ihrer gefährlichsten Stelle, zwischen dem Bäzberg und dem Chilchberg, wo das Wasser eine tiefe Rinne in den Granit gespült hatte. Es dürfte ein einfacher Holzsteg gewesen

writer and winner of the Nobel Prize for Literature, identified in his book on the Gotthard from 1897. 'That was where the gateway was, but nature alone had closed that gate, and nature had not left the key in the lock.' Indeed, even after the fall of the Roman Empire and the beginning of migration in Europe, the wild rocky ravine of the Schöllenen Gorge was to remain an insurmountable obstacle for many centuries and could only be bypassed via slow and perilous mountain paths. Those who wanted to travel directly north from Ticino to Disentis opted for the well-trodden Lukmanierpass. The fastest route to the Valais in the west led over the Simplon. So it was that the German kings and emperors also preferred to take other Alpine passes on their journey to Rome. From the south, the Gotthard was only used by Ticino shepherds who brought their animals to graze in the verdant mountain meadows beyond the pass.

The difficult situation at the Gotthard only changed in the High Middle Ages. There has been much speculation as to what sparked the development of the Schöllenen and thus the creation of the Gotthard Pass in the 12th century, a good 1,000 years after the construction of the Roman Alpine Roads. Was it the agricultural revolution around the year 1100, which led to the growing specialisation and division of labour among the Uri peasants that gave rise to the principle of alpine farming, making local trade between the previously isolated mountain valleys prosper? Did the arrival of the Rapperswil folk in the canton of Uri and the sudden boom in population prompt the new valley dwellers to move further up into the mountains and encourage them to make contact with their neighbours on the other side of the summit? Was it the religious rulers like the monastery of Disentis, to whom the Ursern Valley belonged, or the Bishop of Milan, which had consecrated a chapel on the pass between 1166 and 1176, which now wanted to expand its sphere of influence? The reasons may never be completely revealed. The story is somewhat different for the also rather difficult question of who ultimately established the pass. There is now much to suggest that it was the famous Walser people who migrated from Valais and the Bernese Oberland via the Furka to the Ursern Valley, who used their experiences from the construction of high alpine paths and bridges between the years 1190 and 1230 to make the Schöllenen passable. The Uri landowners on the northern slopes of the gorge must have also supported their new German-speaking neighbours in the project, and thus not only gained access to the crucial Alpine meadows but opened up new trade markets in Leventina and Lombardy to sell their products.

In order to open up the Gotthard Pass, the Reuss River first had to be spanned at its most dangerous point between the Bäzberg and the Chilchberg, where the water had gouged a deep groove into the granite. It would have been a simple wooden footbridge which allowed the

first wayfarers to cross the roaring torrents. The spray from the wild roiling Reuss, swollen after heavy rainfall or during snowmelt and completely shrouded in cold, damp fog earned, the bridge the name Stiebende Steg (spray bridge). It was not until the 16th century that the bridge became known as the Devil's Bridge beyond the country's borders – more about this later. The unnamed constructors, however, managed to create an architectural masterpiece a little further upstream with the so-called Twärrenbrücke (plank bridge) at the upper Schöllenen gate. Following the example of the Walser irrigation canals, they constructed a narrow gallery made of planks around the Chilchberg rock, which – supported by chains and beams driven into the rock – was suspended above the abyss. The key to the Schöllenen was found, and the gate swung open.

At first, the new pass crossing would likely have been of local importance and was used by the Uri and Ursern people. However, the new Alpine pass was too attractive to go unnoticed for long. 'The use could not have been a slow, gradual, drop by drop process, then rivulet by rivulet to a stream,' speculated Carl Spitteler, 'but rather like ants that had unexpectedly discovered a new hole in the pantry, marching in a steady procession.' With the opening up of the Schöllenen, the journey over the Gotthard, however, was by no means an easy undertaking. More bridges needed to be built, and only gradually did the existing sections of the bridle path, over which merchants transported their wares, become developed by local communities. The wooden Twärrenbrücke, which iced up from the water spray in winter and required ongoing repairs due to rotting in the summers, had not made the Schöllenen Gorge any less terrifying.

The list of dangers to which wanderers and traders were exposed was long: depending on the season and the weather, rockfalls, landslides and avalanches threatened. Severe gales, violent thunderstorms and sudden cold snaps were as feared as the wild animals that roamed the Ursern Valley. The climb to the top of the pass was also steep and hazardous. When the snowmelt came, the Tremola Gorge on the south slope of the pass with its mighty avalanches caused fear and trepidation. Since the pass remained open throughout the year, innumerable lives were lost on the Gotthard over the centuries. It was mostly faith that gave travellers protection and hope: in the year 1230, the Milanese Archbishop Enrico di Settala dedicated the chapel at the top of the pass to the Low German Saint Godehard, patron saint of merchants and wayfarers. It only took a few decades for the name to become synonymous with the mountain range and the pass crossing, previously known as the Urserenberg. Thus, Saint Gotthard received its name. Around the year 1237, a hospice was added to the pass chapel in which pilgrims and traders could find food and shelter from the weather for the night on their way over the Gotthard.

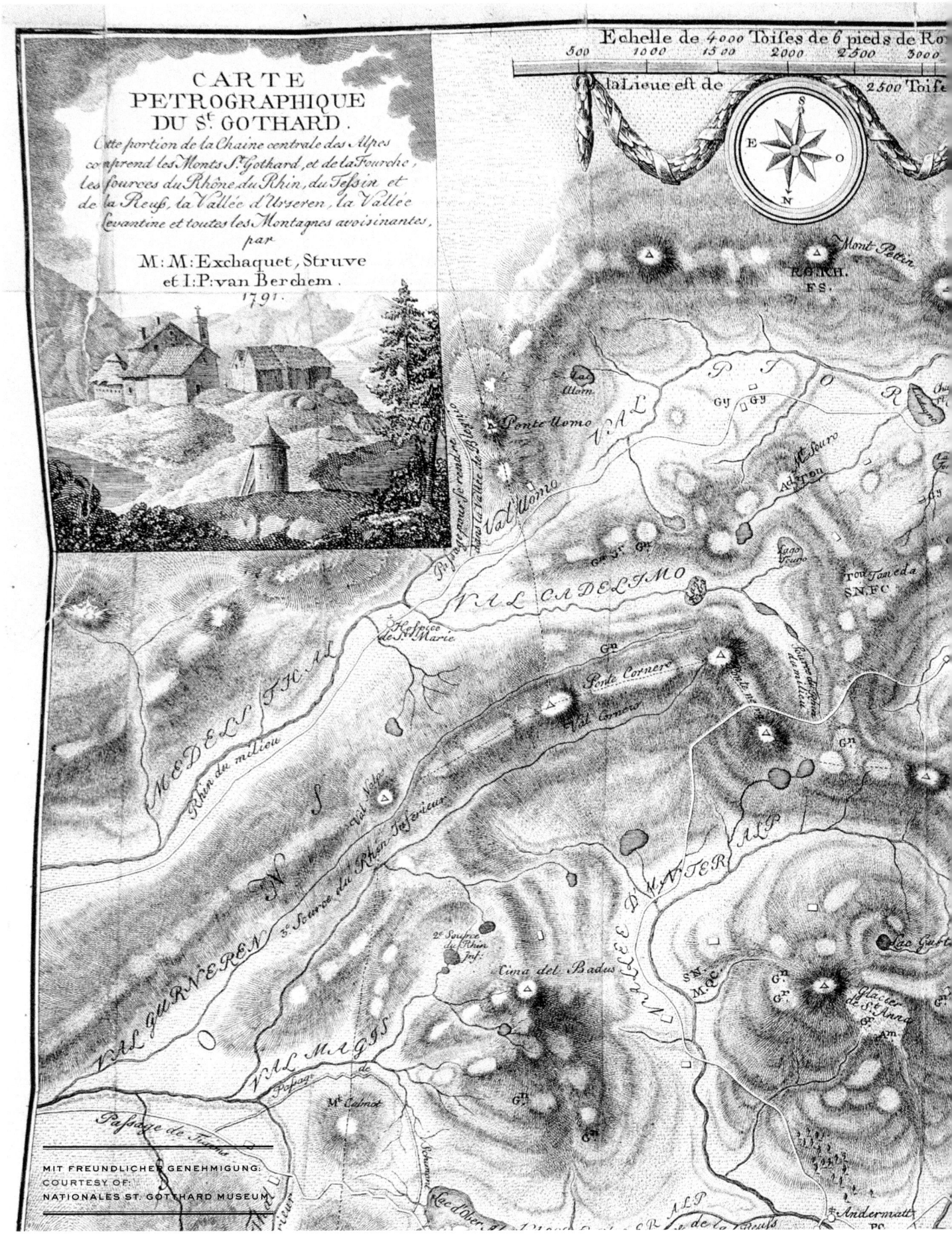

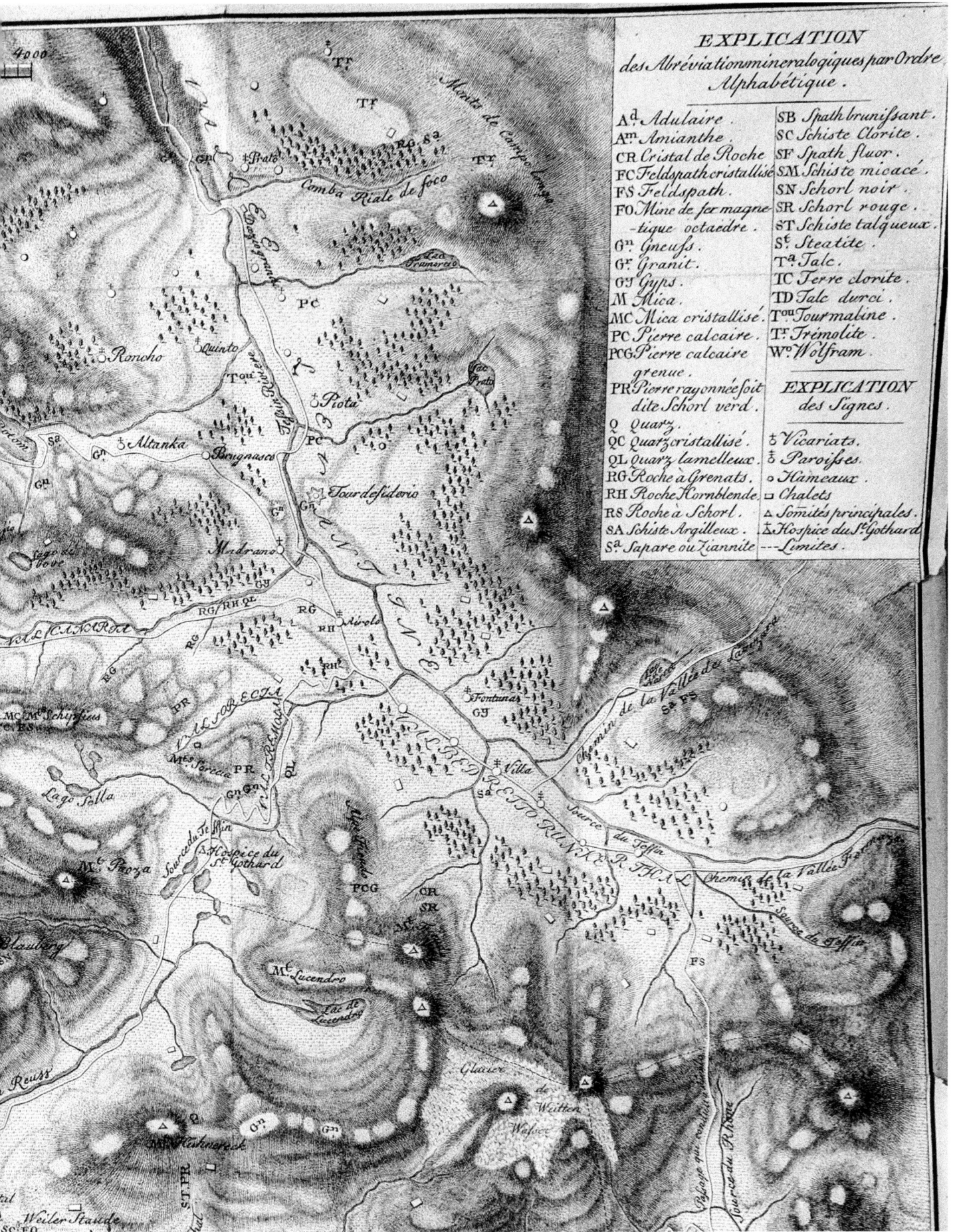

übergang ein – der Sankt Gotthard hatte seinen Namen erhalten. Um das Jahr 1237 existierte neben der Passkapelle zudem ein Hospiz, in dem Pilger und Händler auf ihrem Weg über den Gotthard Schutz vor dem Wetter, Verpflegung und ein Lager für die Nacht finden konnten.

Der Gotthard und die Entstehung der Eidgenossenschaft

Für die wirtschaftlichen Beziehungen zwischen den Talschaften von Uri und der Leventina sowie den wohlhabenden Städten im Norden und Süden gewann der Gotthardpass rasant an Bedeutung. Der Handel mit Fleisch, Milch, Käse und Leder blühte auf – und mit ihm die gesamte Region entlang der Gotthardroute. Es ist kein Zufall, dass sich die Gründungsgeschichte der Schweizerischen Eidgenossenschaft räumlich und zeitlich mit der Erschließung und Etablierung des Gotthardpasses als internationaler Handelsweg überschneidet. Während mächtige Adelsfamilien aus Nord und Süd im 13. Jahrhundert ihren Einfluss auf die neue Alpenverbindung zu vergrößern suchten, entwickelte sich in den vom Gotthardverkehr belebten Tälern Uris eine freiheitliche Politik der Selbstbestimmung, die einen entscheidenden Teil zum Zusammenschluss der Schweizerischen Urkantone beitragen sollte.

Nachdem das Herzogsgeschlecht der Zähringer, das im Auftrag deutscher Könige weite Teile der Schweiz kontrollierte, im Jahr 1218 ausgestorben war, strebte die einflussreiche Adelsfamilie der Habsburger, die vom Elsass bis in die Innerschweiz bereits zahlreiche Regionen beherrschte, das Machtvakuum zu füllen und die Kontrolle über die Gotthardroute zu erhalten. In Uri hatten derweil die Grafen von Rapperswil die lokale Herrschaft übernommen, ab 1232 wachten sie zudem über die selbstständige Reichsvogtei des Urserentals. Für das deutsche Reich mit seinen Einflussgebieten jenseits der Alpen hatte Uri seit der Öffnung des Gotthards erheblich an Bedeutung gewonnen. Um die Expansion der aufstrebenden Habsburger zu bremsen und sich die Passage zu sichern, verlieh König Heinrich VII. den Ursern im Jahr 1231 die Reichsunmittelbarkeit – sie unterstanden nun direkt dem Heiligen Römischen Reich. Im Jahr 1240 erhielt auch der Ort Schwyz den Freiheitsbrief. Der habsburgische Einfluss vergrößerte sich derweil, als Rudolf I. 1273 zum deutschen König gekrönt wurde. Als das Kloster Murbach im Jahr 1291 seine Besitztümer in Luzern und der weiteren Umgebung an die Habsburger verkaufte, hielten sie schließlich die Kontrolle über die gesamte nördliche Handelsstraße – von Hauenstein bei Basel bis zur Passhöhe. Alle Wegzölle wurden nun in Luzern vereinigt und schon bald zur wichtigsten Einkommensquelle des Hauses.

Entlang des Saumpfades waren es jedoch die Bewohner der Talschaften, die sich um den Unterhalt und Ausbau der Wege und Stege bemühten, Gasthäuser betrieben und mit dem Saumhandel einen wichtigen Nebener-

The Gotthard and the Creation of the Swiss Confederacy

For the economic relations between the valley communities of Uri and Leventina as well as the prosperous cities in the north and south, the Gotthard Pass rapidly gained importance. The trade of meat, milk, cheese and leather flourished, and with it, the entire region along the Gotthard route. It is no coincidence that the founding history of the Swiss Confederacy overlaps in time and place with the development and establishment of the Gotthard Pass as an international trade route. While the powerful aristocratic families from the north and south sought to increase their influence on the new Alpine link in the 13th century, in the valleys of Uri , which were bustling with traffic from the Gotthard, a liberal policy of autonomy was established, which would contribute significantly to the amalgamation of the original Swiss cantons.

After the Duchy of the House of Zähringen, which controlled large tracts of Switzerland on behalf of German kings, became extinct in 1218, the influential noble family of the Habsburgs, which had dominated numerous regions from Alsace to central Switzerland, aspired to fill the power vacuum and gain control of the Gotthard route. Meanwhile, in Uri, the Counts of Rapperswil had taken over local rule, and from 1232 they also watched over the autonomous bailiwick of the Ursern Valley. For the German Empire, whose influence reached beyond the Alps, Uri had gained considerable importance since the opening of the Gotthard. In order to stem the hungry Habsburgs and secure the passage, King Henry VII granted the Ursern folk imperial immediacy in the year 1231 – they were now directly under the control of the Holy Roman Empire. In 1240, Schwyz also received the charter of freedom. The Habsburgs' arm of influence grew longer when Rudolf I was crowned King of Germany in 1273. When the Murbach Abbey estate and surrounding lands were sold to the Habsburgs in 1291, they finally gained control of the entire northern section of the trade route from Hauenstein near Basel to the top of the pass. All customs duties and tolls were now pooled in Lucerne and soon became the most important source of income for the Royal House.

Along the bridle paths, however, it was the people living in the valleys who made the effort to maintain and expand the paths and footbridges, operate inns, and find an important sideline enterprise for agriculture in the hauling trade. The muleteers organised cooperatives, introduced transport monopolies in their areas, collected cartage and toll fees and built storage warehouses, which were called Susts. In these warehouses, traders could protect their goods from wind and weather, or temporarily store them and speculate on better market prices. Here, they could also exchange and load up their pack animals. The name of the storage facilities came from the weight unit of the maximum load of goods that a horse or mule could carry: a 'sust' corresponds to around 330 pounds or

Die Teuffels Brugg in den Urner Gebürgen auf der Schelenen genannt.

MIT FREUNDLICHER GENEHMIGUNG
COURTESY OF:
KANTON URI STAATSARCHIV

MIT FREUNDLICHER GENEHMIGUNG
COURTESY OF:
KANTON URI STAATSARCHIV

Imp. Lemercier, Paris.

diable
hard.

Charnaux, Place du Bel-Air, M.on des trois Rois à Genève.

Hospice du St Gotthard.

werb zur Landwirtschaft gefunden hatten. Die Säumer organisierten sich genossenschaftlich, führten auf ihren Gebieten Transportmonopole ein, kassierten Fuhrlöhne und Weggebühren, errichteten Warenlager. In den sogenannten Susten konnten Händler ihre Waren vor Wind und Wetter schützen – oder zwischenlagern und auf bessere Marktpreise spekulieren. Hier wurden auch die Saumtiere ausgewechselt und beladen. Der Name der Lager leitete sich von der Gewichtseinheit jener Warenlast ab, die einem Pferd und Maulesel maximal aufgebürdet werden durfte: Eine »Sust« entsprach etwa drei Zentnern oder rund 150 Kilogramm. Die Sustmeister vermerkten auch die Waren, die transportiert wurden. Trugen die Kaufleute aus dem Norden vor allem Käse und Vieh, robuste Stoffe, Pelze, Leder, Salz, Metall und Waffen über den Pass, transportierten die Händler aus dem Süden exotische Luxuswaren wie Seidenstoffe und orientalische Teppiche, die über Venedig nach Italien gelangt waren, aber auch Öl, Gewürze und Wein.

Die Transportgenossenschaften beherrschten zwischen Urnerland und Leventina bald die gesamte Gotthardroute. Und auch die Fährleute auf dem Vierwaldstätter-, dem Langen- und dem Luganersee schlossen sich zu Schifffahrtsgesellschaften zusammen. Die einstmals selbstständigen, von einander abgeschnittenen Täler wuchsen so immer mehr zu Schicksalsgemeinschaften zusammen, die im Sinne ihrer wirtschaftlichen Interessen kooperierten, entlang der Handelsroute für Sicherheit sorgten – und auch ihre eigene Rechtsprechung praktizierten. Um ihre Autonomierechte und den Einfluss über die lukrative Gotthardroute mit ihren Zolleinnahmen zurückzugewinnen, schlossen die am Vierwaldstättersee gelegenen Talschaften Uri, Schwyz und Unterwalden im Jahr 1291 ein neues Landfriedensbündnis. Der Bundesbrief, in dem man sich die gegenseitige Unterstützung zusicherte, gilt als Gründungsdokument der alten Eidgenossenschaft. Aus der Geschichte des Freiheitskämpfers Wilhelm Tell und der Legende vom Rütlischwur – bei dem sich Vertreter von Uri, Schwyz und Unterwalden auf einer Wiese am Vierwaldstättersee die Treue gegen die tyrannischen Vögte der Habsburger schworen und der erstmals 1470 im »Weissen Buch von Sarnen« erwähnt wurde – bildete sich über die Jahrhunderte ein Nationalmythos, in dem der Gotthard als Wiege der Schweiz eine entscheidende Rolle spielte.

Auf der Südseite des Passes war ebenfalls um die Einflusssphäre gerungen worden. Die Bischöfe von Como und das Domkapital von Mailand, bisher die Herrscher über die Passhöhe, befanden sich plötzlich in Konkurrenz mit einflussreichen Mailänder Familien wie den Ruscas und den Viscontis, die im 14. Jahrhundert ihre Macht bis hinauf zur Passhöhe, teils sogar bis ins Urserental ausdehnten. Doch auch die junge Eidgenossenschaft im Norden bemühte sich, immer mehr Kontrolle über den Pass zu erlangen. Nachdem die Habsburger 1313 bei Morgarten eine Niederlage gegen die vereinten Waldstätte

about 150 kilograms. The 'sust master' also made a note of the goods that were being transported. The merchants from the north brought mainly cheese and cattle, robust fabrics, furs, leather, salt, metal and weapons over the pass; the traders from the south brought exotic luxury goods such as silk fabrics and oriental carpets, which had come to Italy via Venice, as well as oil, spices and wine.

The transport cooperatives soon controlled the entire Gotthard route between the canton of Uri and the Leventina district. The ferrymen on the Lucerne, Langen and Lugano lakes also joined forces to form shipping companies. The once independent, isolated valleys pulled closer and closer together to forge communities of destiny, which served them well in their economic interests to work together in keeping the trade route safe and also to mete out their own forms of justice. In order to regain their autonomous rights over the lucrative Gotthard route with its toll revenue, the Uri, Schwyz and Unterwalden valleys abutting Lake Lucerne agreed on a new peace alliance in 1291. The Federal Charter, which assured mutual support, is regarded as the founding document of the Old Swiss Confederacy. The story of the freedom fighter William Tell and the legend of the Rütlischwur – an oath that was first mentioned in 1470 in the White Book of Sarnen, in which representatives of Uri, Schwyz and Unterwalden swore allegiance against the tyrannical governors of the Habsburgs in a meadow on Lake Lucerne – grew over the centuries to become a national myth in which the Gotthard played a leading role as the cradle of Switzerland.

On the south side of the pass, there was also a wrestle for more influence. The bishops of Como and the cathedral chapter of Milan, as the rulers of the pass at that time, suddenly found themselves in competition with influential Milanese families such as the Ruscas and the Viscontis, whose power in the 14th century reached as far as the pass summit and even stretched into the Ursern Valley. However, the fledgling Confederation in the north also sought to gain more and more control over the pass. After the Habsburgs suffered a defeat at Morgarten in 1313 against the unified Confederate allies, the Confederacy began to secure control of the Gotthard route one piece at a time by forging new alliances with Lucerne, Zurich, Glarus, Zug and Bern as well as military advances to the south. The Uri pushed into Leventina and through to Lombardy and Milan. The bitter defeat against the French at Marignano in 1515 finally heralded an end to the expansion and super power aspirations. Nevertheless, with the conquering of the canton of Ticino, the southern doorway to the Gotthard was firmly in Confederacy hands.

Meanwhile, the Confederation had as a state adopted institutional forms and with its 13 cantons also created a network of alliances that would remain intact for the next 300 years. The cantons coordinated their poli-

erlitten und ihre Ambitionen am Gotthard zurückgefahren hatten, begannen die Eidgenossen, die Gotthardroute durch neue Bündnisse mit Luzern, Zürich, Glarus, Zug und Bern sowie militärische Vorstöße nach Süden Stück für Stück abzusichern und unter ihre Kontrolle zu bringen. Die Urner stießen dabei in die Leventina und durch die Lombardei bis nach Mailand vor. Erst 1515 beendete eine herbe Niederlage gegen die Franzosen bei Marignano die Expansions- und Großmachtbestrebungen. Dennoch lag mit dem Tessin fortan das südliche Tor zum Gotthard fest in eidgenössischer Hand.

Die Eidgenossenschaft hatte unterdessen als Staatswesen institutionelle Formen angenommen – und mit 13 Länderorten auch ein Bündnisgeflecht geschaffen, das die kommenden 300 Jahre bestehen bleiben sollte. Die Orte koordinierten ihre Politik an sogenannten Tagsatzungen, zu denen sie Gesandte schickte. Neben den ansehnlichen Zoll- und Transporteinnahmen aus dem Saumverkehr über den Pass profitierten die eidgenössischen Talschaften und Städte mittlerweile vom lukrativen Geschäft mit Söldnern und Armeen, die gegen Gebühr an ausländische Machthaber verliehen wurden. Die wechselnden Soldbündnisse dienten auch als Schutz für den Verkehrsweg über den Gotthard – kein Land wollte sich die Möglichkeit versperren, im Kriegsfall auf Schweizer Söldner zurückgreifen zu können.

Die Sage von der Teufelsbrücke

Im 16. Jahrhundert bahnte sich die Reformation von Zürich und Genf aus ihren Weg durch die Schweiz, es kam vermehrt zu Konflikten zwischen den katholischen Urkantonen und den reformierten Städten und Regionen. Was die Konfessionen einte, war die Furcht vor dem Leibhaftigen – und der zeigte sich auf der »Straße des Schreckens« am Gotthard in mannigfaltiger Form. Schon früher hatten sich reisende Geistliche die Augen verbinden lassen, um den Gefahren der »erschröcklichen« Bergwelt nicht ins Auge blicken zu müssen. Ein Chronist aus Bologna riet 1558 gar, den »Stiebenden Steg« nur auf allen Vieren zu überqueren. Und im Jahr 1587 berichtete ein Basler Kaufmann nach dem »Gang durch die Hölle«, der Schöllenen habe das grasreiche, flache Urserental auf ihn wie das Paradies gewirkt. Acht Jahre später wurde die vormals hölzerne Brücke, die in der Schöllenenschlucht die Reus überquerte, aus Stein neu errichtet. Etwa zur gleichen Zeit verbreitete sich die Kunde, der Teufel habe beim Bau der ersten Brücke seine Hände im Spiel gehabt.

Die Geschichte ging so: Verzweifelt hätten die Urner einst versucht, über die tosenden Fluten der Reuss einen Steg zu schlagen. »Do sell der Tyfel e Brigg bue!«, habe der Landammann als Vorsitzender der Gemeinde schließlich geschrien – und natürlich hatte sich der Teufel nicht lange bitten lassen. Der Leibhaftige schlug den Urnern einen Deal vor: Er baue die Brücke, erhalte als

cies in a so-called Tagsatzungen (federal diet), to which they sent representatives. In addition to the considerable customs and transport revenue from muleteer traffic over the pass, the valleys and cities of the Confederacy had profited from the lucrative business of mercenaries and armies, which were loaned to foreign powers for a fee. The changing pact coalitions also served as protection for the transport route over the Gotthard – no country wanted to close the door to obtaining the services of Swiss mercenaries in the event of war.

The Legend of the Devil's Bridge

In the 16th century, the Reformation spread from Zurich and Geneva through Switzerland and increasing conflicts erupted between the original cantons and the reformed cities and regions. What united the denominations was the fear of the devil – and this manifested itself in many forms along the 'road of terror' at the Gotthard. Even in earlier times, travelling clerics would be blindfolded so they would not have to face the horrors of the frightening mountainous world. In 1558, a chronicler from Bologna even advised wayfarers to cross the wooden Stiebende Steg on all fours. And in 1587, a merchant from Basel reported that after his 'passage through hell', the Schöllenen made the grassy, flat Ursern Valley seem like paradise. Eight years later, the wooden bridge that spanned the Reuss in the Schöllenen Gorge was rebuilt out of stone. At about the same time, news spread that the devil had had a hand in the construction of the first bridge.

The story went like this: the Uri folk had desperately tried to cobble a footbridge over the roaring torrents of the Reuss. One day in desperation, a Landammann or canton chief cried: 'Do sell der Tyfel e Brigg bue' (let the devil build a bridge here) – and, of course, the devil didn't need to be asked twice. Satan offered the people of Uri a deal: he would build the bridge, but in return he would take the soul of the first to cross it. The clever Uri folk sent a goat across the bridge, which in turn so infuriated the cloven-hoofed lord of darkness that he was determined to smash the bridge to pieces with a rock. In this rock, however, a pious woman had chiselled out a crucifix. This puzzled the devil so much that he missed his target and the boulder landed in the Schöllenen Gorge. From then on, the Stiebende Steg was known as the Devil's Bridge. As a visually stunning symbol of mankind's victory over the horrors of the mountains, this bridge has inspired generations of poets and artists. Eventually, almost four centuries later, the duped Beelzebub received some belated satisfaction when, in 1973, the 2,000-tonne devil's rock had to be moved 127 metres for a price of 300,000 Swiss Francs in order to make way for the new Gotthard autobahn.

In addition to trade, the postal service over the Gotthard became increasingly important in the 17th century. Be-

Gegenleistung aber die Seele jenes Unglücklichen, der sie als Erstes überquere. Die schlauen Urner aber schickten einen Geissbock hinüber, was wiederum den ziegenfüßigen Herr der Finsternis derart erzürnte, dass er die Brücke mit einem Felsen zertrümmern wollte. In diesen aber hatte ein gottesfürchtiges Mütterchen ein Kreuz geritzt. Dies wiederum verwirrte den Teufel derart, dass er sein Ziel verfehlte und der Brocken in der Schöllenenschlucht landete. Der »stiebende Steg« ward fortan als Teufelsbrücke bekannt. Als bildgewaltiges Symbol für den Sieg des Menschen über die Schrecken der Bergwelt inspirierte sie Generationen von Dichtern und Künstlern. Späte Genugtuung erhielt der übel geprellte Beelzebub übrigens fast vier Jahrhunderte später, als im Jahr 1973 der rund 2.000 Tonnen schwere Teufelsstein für 300.000 Franken um 127 Meter verschoben werden musste, um der neuen Gotthard-Autobahn zu weichen.

Neben dem Handel gewann im 17. Jahrhundert auch der Postverkehr über den Gotthard an Bedeutung. Zwischen Basel und Mailand sowie Zürich und Bergamo verkehrte einmal pro Woche ein Fußbote, ab 1630 sorgten berittene Postboten für eine erhöhte Frequenz und kürzere Reisezeit. Mit zunehmendem Schnellverkehr wurden weitere Modernisierungen der Strecke notwendig. Im Jahr 1649 wurde die Händerlisbrücke am unteren Eingang der Schöllenenschlucht aus Stein neu gebaut – sie sollte mehr als 300 Jahre bestehen bleiben. Das nächste Schlüsselbauwerk in der Geschichte des Gotthardpasses entstand jedoch erst Anfang des 18. Jahrhunderts. Inzwischen war der Warenverkehr über den Gotthard vollständig professionalisiert worden und äußerst ertragreich für die lokale Bevölkerung. Dennoch erhöhten die Urner immer wieder die Zölle – und mussten schließlich mit ansehen, wie die Händler in Scharen auf die günstigeren Pässe Graubündens auswichen. Die »Gotthardkrise« erhöhte den Druck auf die Urner Stände, den Alpenübergang für den Handel wieder attraktiv zu machen. Und das ließ sich am besten bewerkstelligen, indem man die Reisezeit deutlich verkürzte. Eine der Engstellen des Passes war die Twerrenbrücke, die von Pferden nur widerwillig passiert wurde und die derart oft ausgebessert werden musste, dass die Wälder des Urserentals langsam, aber sicher ihrer Instandhaltung zum Opfer fielen. Zähneknirschend entschieden sich die Urner, den Plan des Tessiner Baumeisters Pietro Morettini umzusetzen, ein Budget freizugeben und mit Schwarzpulver einen Tunnel in den Chilchberg zu sprengen. Im August 1708, rund 500 Jahre nach der Überbrückung der Schöllenen, eröffnete das 64 Meter lange »Urnerloch« – als erster Tunnelbau der Alpen.

Der Tunnel läutete ein neues Kapitel in der Geschichte des Gotthardpasses ein. Für beschleunigten Warentransport und eine schnellere Abwicklung sorgte auch ein 1708 geschlossenes Abkommen über einheitliche Sustgelder und Fürleitgebühren, die Händler mit eigenen Transporttieren für Passage und freies Geleit zu zahlen

tween Basel and Milan as well as Zurich and Bergamo, postal carriers delivered mail once a week on foot. From 1630, mounted postmen provided more regular deliveries in a shorter time. With the increasing speed of traffic, further modernisation of the route became necessary. In 1649, the Händerlis Bridge at the lower entrance of the Schöllenen Gorge was rebuilt out of stone and it would remain like this for more than 300 years. However, the next key construction project in the history of the Gotthard Pass was not undertaken until the beginning of the 18th century. Meanwhile, the movement of goods over the Gotthard had become professionalised and extremely lucrative for the local population. Nevertheless, the Uri folk continued to raise customs duties and eventually could only look on as droves of traders avoided the Gotthard in preference to the cheaper passes through the Grisons. The 'Gotthard crisis' increased the pressure on the Uri canton to again make the crossing of the Alps more attractive to traders and this was best done by shortening the travel time significantly. One of the bottlenecks of the pass was the Twärrenbrücke, which was only reluctantly traversed with horses and had to undergo so many repairs that the forests of the Ursern Valley slowly but surely disappeared to maintain the bridge. With much gnashing of the teeth, the Uri canton decided to implement the plan of the Ticinese architect, Pietro Morettini, to approve a budget to take gunpowder and blast a tunnel into the Chilchberg. In August 1708, around 500 years after the bridging of the Schöllenen, the 64-metre-long 'Urnerloch' opened – the first tunnel construction in the Alps.

The tunnel heralded a new chapter in the history of the Gotthard Pass. For speedier transport of goods and faster processing, an agreement was made in 1708 on a standardised Sust payment and rate for fees that the traders had to pay for the passage and safe convoy when using their own pack animals. Moreover, from 1720 onwards, a new, central pack-transport regulation came into force, which remained valid until the early 19th century. By 1750, the annual volume of goods transported over the Gotthard by pack animals in summertime and by ox sleds in winter had reached more than 2,600 tonnes. The first horse-drawn wagons also appeared at the Gotthard around this time: however, legend has it that an English geologist, who wanted to be the first to conquer the old mule track with a carriage, insisted that 78 men disassemble the carriage in the narrow passages and reassemble them again on the other side.

The Mental Conquest of the Alps

Expediting the traffic on the Gotthard Pass was the vaulting of the mental hurdle of the Alps. While the alpine regions were once considered a haven of terror, scientists, artists and writers from all over Europe, illuminated by the spirit of enlightenment, discovered the mountainscape. From 1755, the Geneva-based nat-

ONTAGNE DE St GOTTHARD D'URY

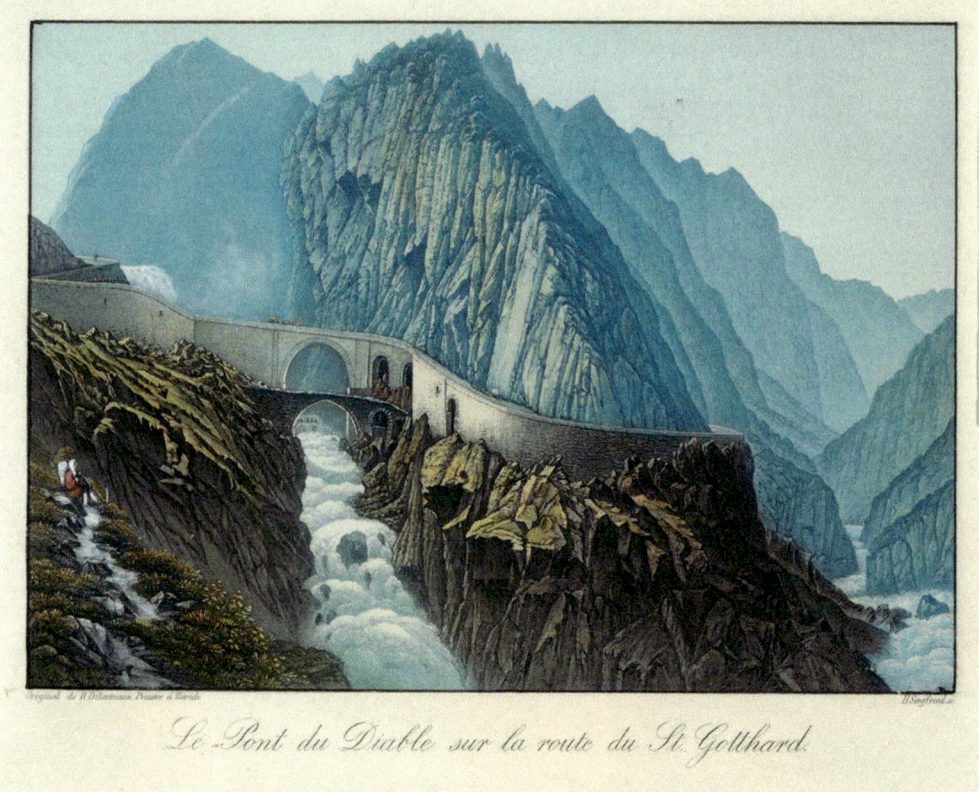

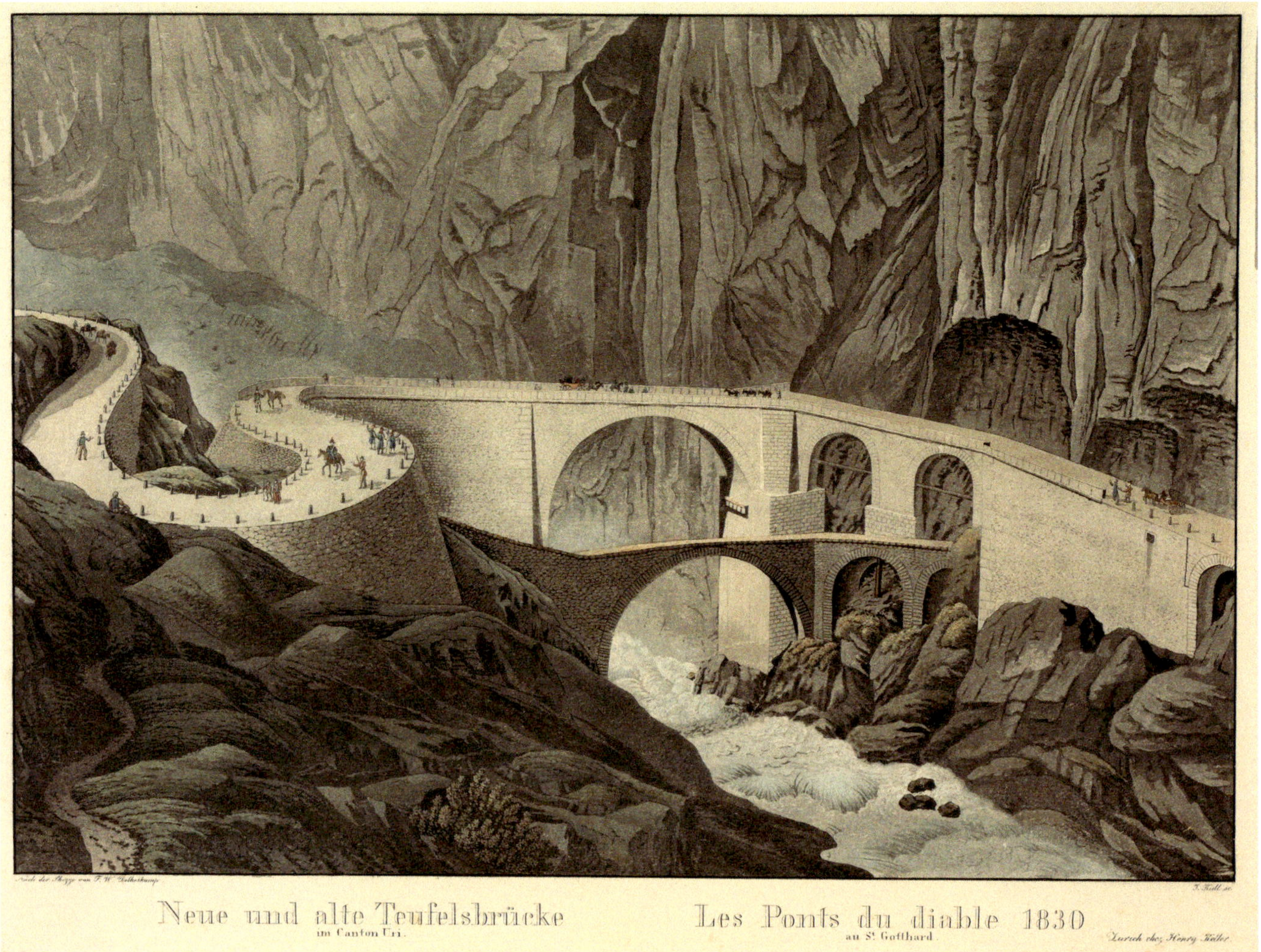
Neue und alte Teufelsbrücke
im Canton Uri.
Les Ponts du diable 1830
au St. Gotthard.
Zurich chez Henry Keller.

MIT FREUNDLICHER GENEHMIGUNG
COURTESY OF:
KANTON URI STAATSARCHIV

Le Pont du Diable sur la route du St. Gotthard.

TÜFELSBRUGG.
Auf dem Gotthart, Urner Gebiet.

TÜFELSBROUGG.
Pont sur le Gotthart, au Canton d'Urij.

hatten. Ab 1720 trat zudem eine neue, zentrale Saumordnung in Kraft, die bis ins frühe 19. Jahrhundert bestehen blieb. Um 1750 lag die jährliche Warenmenge, die im Sommer auf Saumtieren und im Winter per Ochsenschlitten über den Gotthard transportiert wurde, bei rund 2.600 Tonnen. Auch die ersten Pferdewagen tauchten zu dieser Zeit am Gotthard auf: Jener englische Geologe, der den alten Saumweg als Erster mit einer Kutsche befahren wollte, benötigte der Überlieferung nach allerdings 78 Helfer, um das Gefährt an Engstellen demontieren und im Anschluss wieder zusammensetzen zu lassen.

Die mentale Eroberung der Alpen

Zur Beschleunigung des Passverkehrs am Gotthard kam die mentale Eroberung der Alpen. Hatten die Hochgebirge einst als Hort des Schreckens gegolten, entdeckten nun vom Geist der Aufklärung erhellte Wissenschaftler, Künstler und Literaten in ganz Europa die Bergwelt für sich. Ab 1755 führte der Genfer Naturforscher Horace Bénédict de Saussure im Gotthardmassiv erste barometrische Höhenmessungen durch – und stieß den Gotthard als höchsten Berg Europas vom Thron. Sein ab 1779 erscheinene Buchreihe »Voyages dans les Alpes« sollte zum Standardwerk der neuen Alpenforschung werden. Der Begeisterung für die erhabene Bergwelt folgte auch Johann Wolfgang von Goethe. Zwischen 1775 und 1797 besuchte der Dichter auf seinen Schweizer Reisen gleich drei Mal den Gotthardpass. »Der Gotthard ist zwar nicht das höchste Gebirg der Schweiz, und in Savoyen übertrifft ihn der Montblanc an Höhe um sehr vieles; doch behauptet er den Rang eines königlichen Gebirges über alle andere, weil die größten Gebirgsketten bei ihm zusammen laufen und sich an ihn lehnen«, so berichtete Goethe 1775 in seinen Briefen aus der Schweiz. Den tatsächlichen Aufstieg empfand der Dichter dann wohl nicht mehr ganz so erbaulich: »Noth und Müh und Schweis«, notiert er in sein Tagebuch und beschreibt die Schöllenenschlucht jenseits der Teufelsbrücke als »öde wie in Thale des Todts – mit Gebeinen besäet«. An der Passhöhe wagte er zwar den »Scheideblick nach Italien« und hält die Aussicht in Zeichnungen fest – machte jedoch bei allen drei Besuchen kehrt. Dennoch trug Goethe wohl maßgeblich zur Verbreitung des Gotthardmythos bei: Nach seiner letzten Reise berichtete Goethe seinem Freund Friedrich von Schiller von der Sage des Volkshelden Wilhelm Tell, die ihm am Vierwaldstättersee zugetragen worden war. 1804 veröffentlichte Schiller sein gleichnamiges Drama, das zum Grundstein des modernen Schweizer Nationalmythos werden sollte.

Die dramatisch-düstere Schöllenenschlucht mit ihrer Teufelsbrücke wurde indes zum neuen Sehnsuchtsort der Romantik. In seinem »Berglied« dichtete Schiller, der den Gotthard selbst nur aus Erzählungen kannte: »Es schwebt eine Brücke hoch über den Rand. / Der furchtbaren Tiefe gebogen / Sie ward nicht erbauet von Menschenhand / Es hätte sichs keines verwogen / Der Strom

uralist Horace Bénédict de Saussure conducted the first barometric altitude measurements in the massif – and shoved the Gotthard, as Europe's highest mountain, off its throne. His book series Voyages dans les Alpes published from 1779 would become the standard reference for new Alpine research. Johann Wolfgang von Goethe also became smitten with the majestic mountain world. Between 1775 and 1797, the writer visited the Gotthard Pass three times during his journeys through Switzerland. 'The Gotthard, indeed, is not the highest mountain of Switzerland; in Savoy, Mont Blanc has a far higher elevation and yet it maintains above all others the rank of king of mountains, because all the great chains converge together around him, and all rest upon him as their base,' the scribe wrote in his letters from Switzerland in 1775. Alas, Goethe was less enthusiastic about the actual climb: 'Misery and pain and sweat,' he noted in his diary, and described the Schöllenen Gorge beyond the Devil's Bridge as 'desolate as the Valley of Death – littered with bones.' At the top of the pass, he caught a 'glimpse of Italy' and captured the view in drawings – but turned back on all three occasions. Still, Goethe obviously contributed greatly to the spreading of the Gotthard myth: after his last trip, Goethe told his friend Friedrich von Schiller about the legend of the popular hero William Tell, which he had heard at Vierwaldstättersee. In 1804, Schiller published his eponymous drama, which would become the cornerstone of the modern Swiss national myth.

The dramatically gloomy Schöllenen Gorge with its Devil's Bridge became the new place of yearning for the romantic era. Von Schiller, who only knew the Gotthard from hearsay, wrote in his 'Song of the Alps': That bridge with its dizzying, perilous span / Aloft o'er the gulf and its flood suspended / Think'st thou it was built by the art of man / By his hand that grim old arch was bended? / Far down in the jaws of the gloomy abyss / The water is boiling and hissing, – forever will hiss. William Turner, the great English Romantic landscape artist, captured the Devil's Bridge in 1802 in an impressive painting – thus inspiring many passing travellers to stop at the Gotthard on their journeys across Europe. They revelled in the beauty of the rugged mountainscape and dreamt of a simple life in harmony with nature. Switzerland was reborn as a tourist destination.

The Rocky Road to Neutrality

However, the Gotthard also attracted less sophisticated visitors. After the French Revolution, the fledgling French Republic invaded its Swiss neighbour in 1798; the 'Helvetic Republic' was proclaimed. Russia and Austria joined forces against revolutionary France and carried the war into Swiss territory. In September 1799, on the back of defeating the French in northern Italy, the Russian General Suvorov stood with more than 21,000 soldiers at the southern foot of the Gotthard in Airolo and loaded mules and Cossack horses with luggage, rations

braust unter ihr spat und früh / Speit ewig hinauf und zertrümmert sie nie.« Auch William Turner, der große englische Künstler und Pionier der Romantik, hielt 1802 die »Devil's Bridge« in einem eindrücklichen Gemälde fest – und inspirierte so zahlreiche Schnellreisende, auf ihren Fahrten durch Europa am Gotthard Station zu machen. Diese ergötzen sich, von wohligen Schauern durchzuckt, an der Erhabenheit der schroffen Bergwelt und träumten von einem einfachen Leben im Einklang mit der Natur. Die Schweiz war als Tourismusdestination neu geboren worden.

Der steinige Weg zur Neutralität

Doch der Gotthard zog auch andere, weniger feingeistige Gäste an. Nach der Französischen Revolution überfiel die junge Französische Republik 1798 ihren eidgenössischen Nachbarn, die »Helvetische Republik« wurde ausgerufen. Russland und Österreich verbündeten sich gegen das revolutionäre Frankreich – und trugen den Krieg auch auf Schweizer Boden. Im September 1799 stand der russische General Suworow nach großen Erfolgen gegen die Franzosen in Norditalien mit mehr als 21.000 Soldaten am südlichen Fuß des Gotthards in Airolo und ließ Maultiere und Kosakenpferde mit Gepäck, Verpflegung und Kanonen beladen. Er hatte Befehl erhalten, die Alpen zu queren, sich bei Zürich mit der russisch-österreichischen Streitmacht zu vereinen und die französischen Besatzer aus der Schweiz zu verjagen.

Bei Nebel, Regen und Kälte begann der mühevolle Aufstieg auf den Gotthard. In der Tremolaschlucht stießen die bergunerfahrenen Soldaten auf den Widerstand französischer Truppen, die sich auf

Hatten die Hochgebirge einst als Hort des Schreckens gegolten, entdeckten nun vom Geist der Aufklärung erhellte Wissenschaftler, Künstler und Literaten in ganz Europa die Bergwelt für sich. Ab 1755 führte der Genfer Naturforscher Horace Bénédict de Saussure im Gotthardmassiv erste barometrische Höhenmessungen durch – und stieß den Gotthard als höchsten Berg Europas vom Thron.

While the alpine regions were once considered a haven of terror, scientists, artists and writers from all over Europe, illuminated by the spirit of enlightenment, discovered the mountainscape. From 1755, the Geneva-based naturalist Horace Bénédict de Saussure conducted the first barometric altitude measurements in the massif – and shoved the Gotthard, as Europe's highest mountain, off its throne.

and canons. He had received the order to cross the Alps, to join up with the Russian-Austrian forces near Zurich, and to drive the French occupiers out of Switzerland.

In fog, rain and chilly temperatures, the laborious Gotthard ascent began. In the Tremola Gorge, the soldiers, who were woefully inexperienced in mountaineering, countered resistance from the French troops who had entrenched themselves at the top of the pass. Suvorov's soldiers, however, managed to take the hospice and push the enemies back, first through the Ursern Valley and finally – after fierce battles which partially destroyed the Devil's Bridge – out of the Schöllenen. Arriving in Altdorf, Suvorov finally realised, however, that the route he'd expected along the Vierwaldstätter-

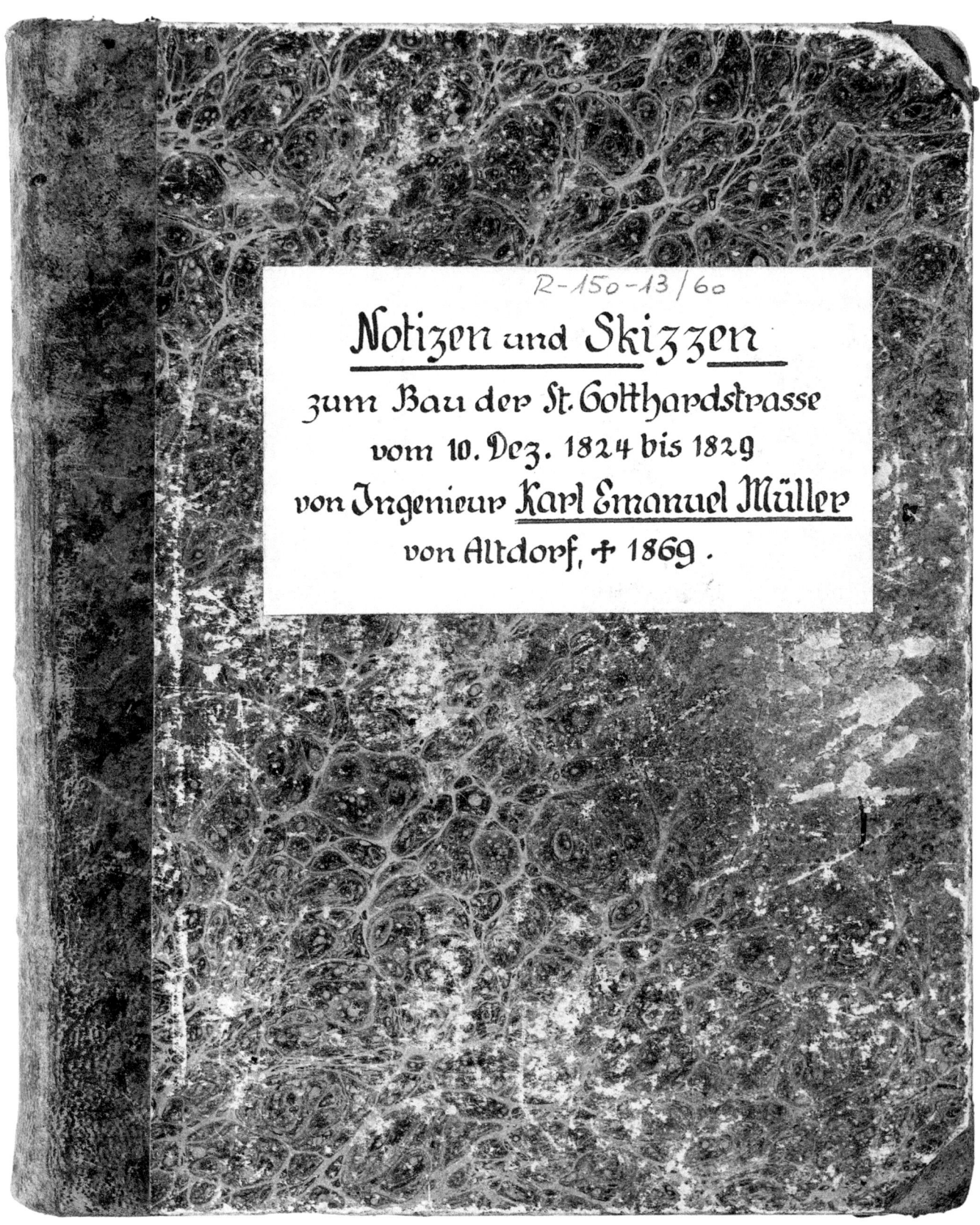

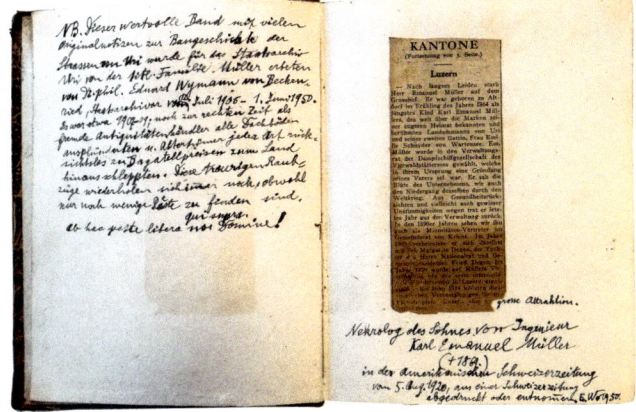

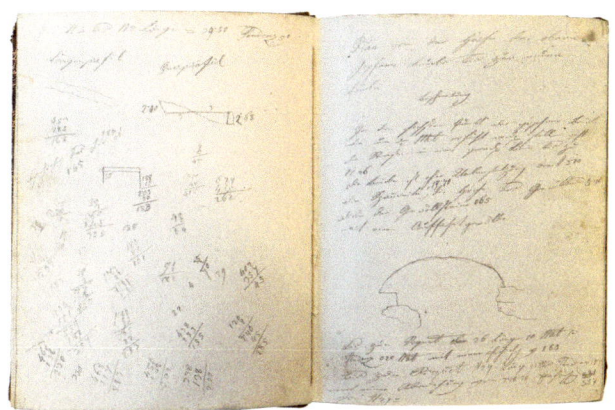
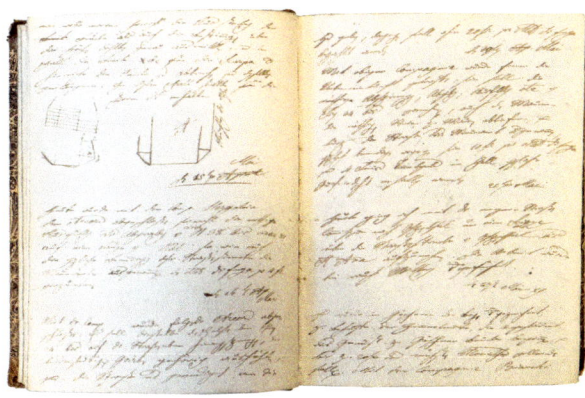
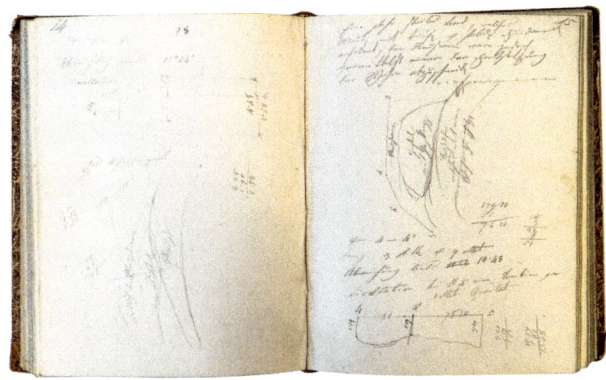
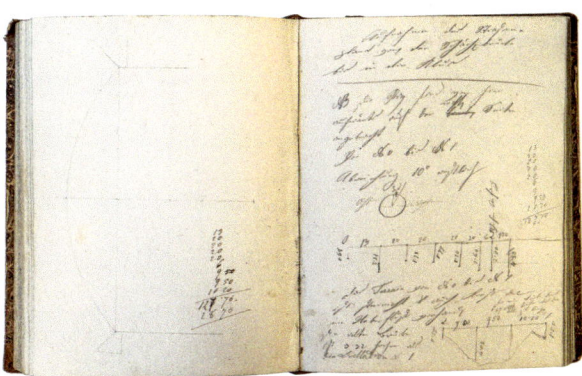

MIT FREUNDLICHER GENEHMIGUNG
COURTESY OF:
KANTON URI STAATSARCHIV

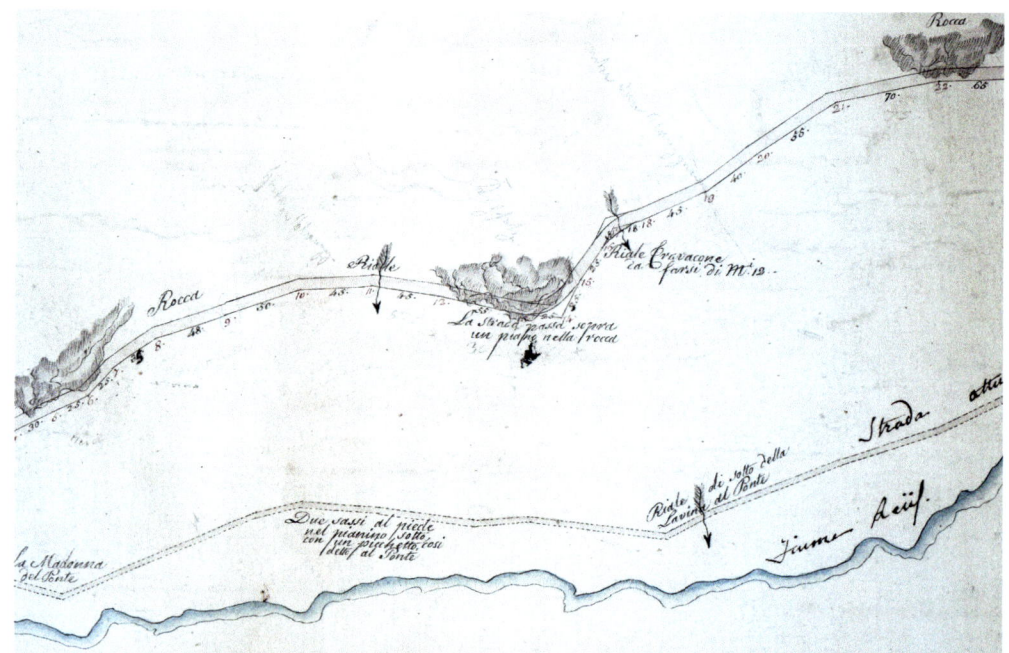

MIT FREUNDLICHER GENEHMIGUNG
COURTESY OF:
KANTON URI STAATSARCHIV

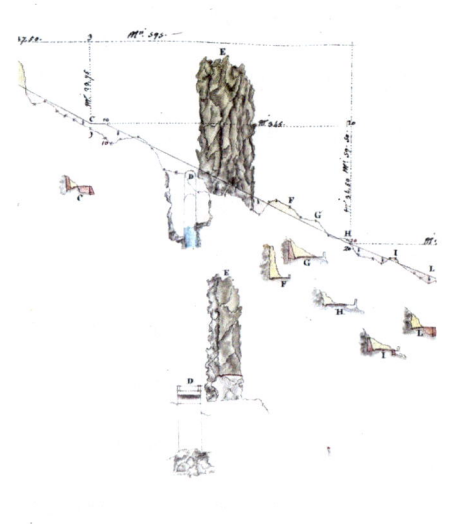

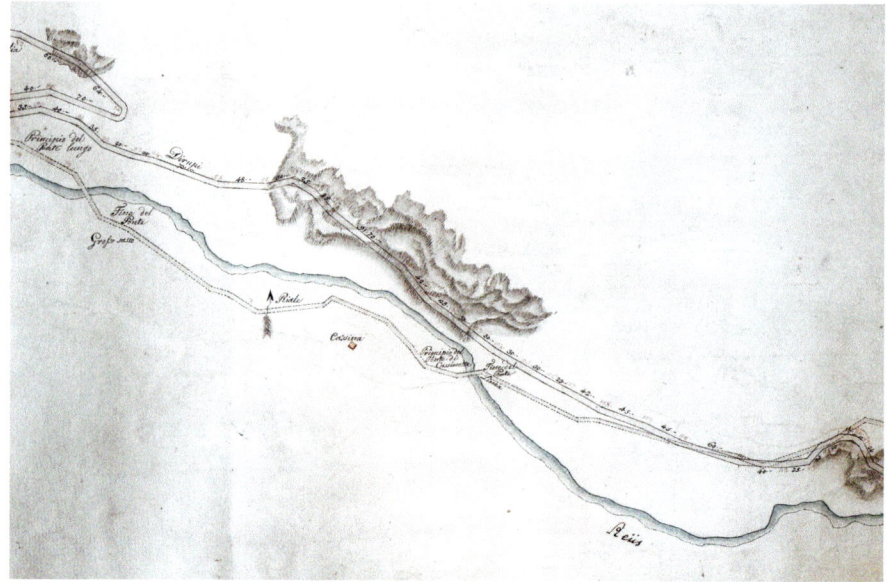

42 — GESCHICHTE / HISTORY

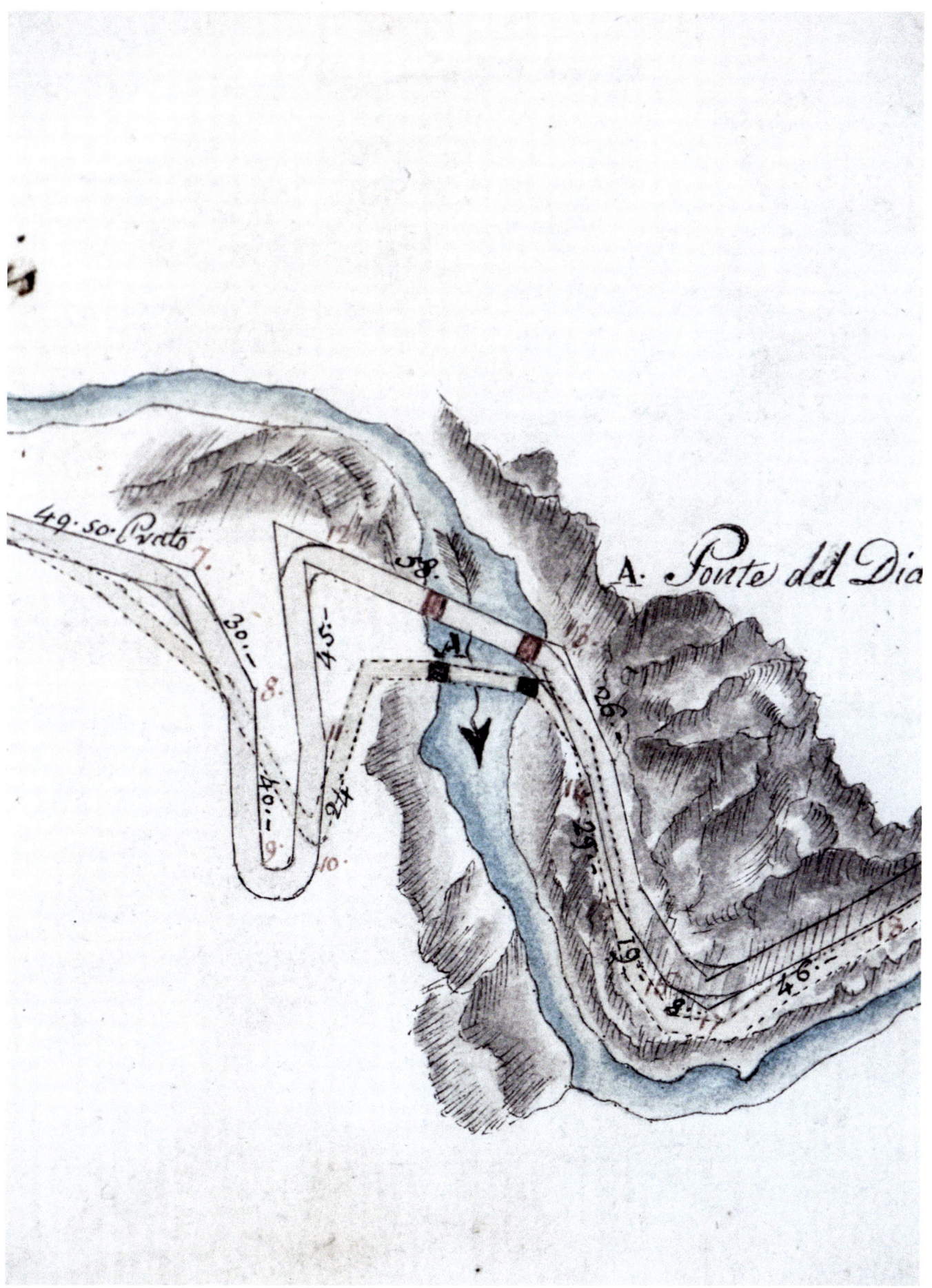

MIT FREUNDLICHER GENEHMIGUNG
COURTESY OF:
KANTON URI STAATSARCHIV

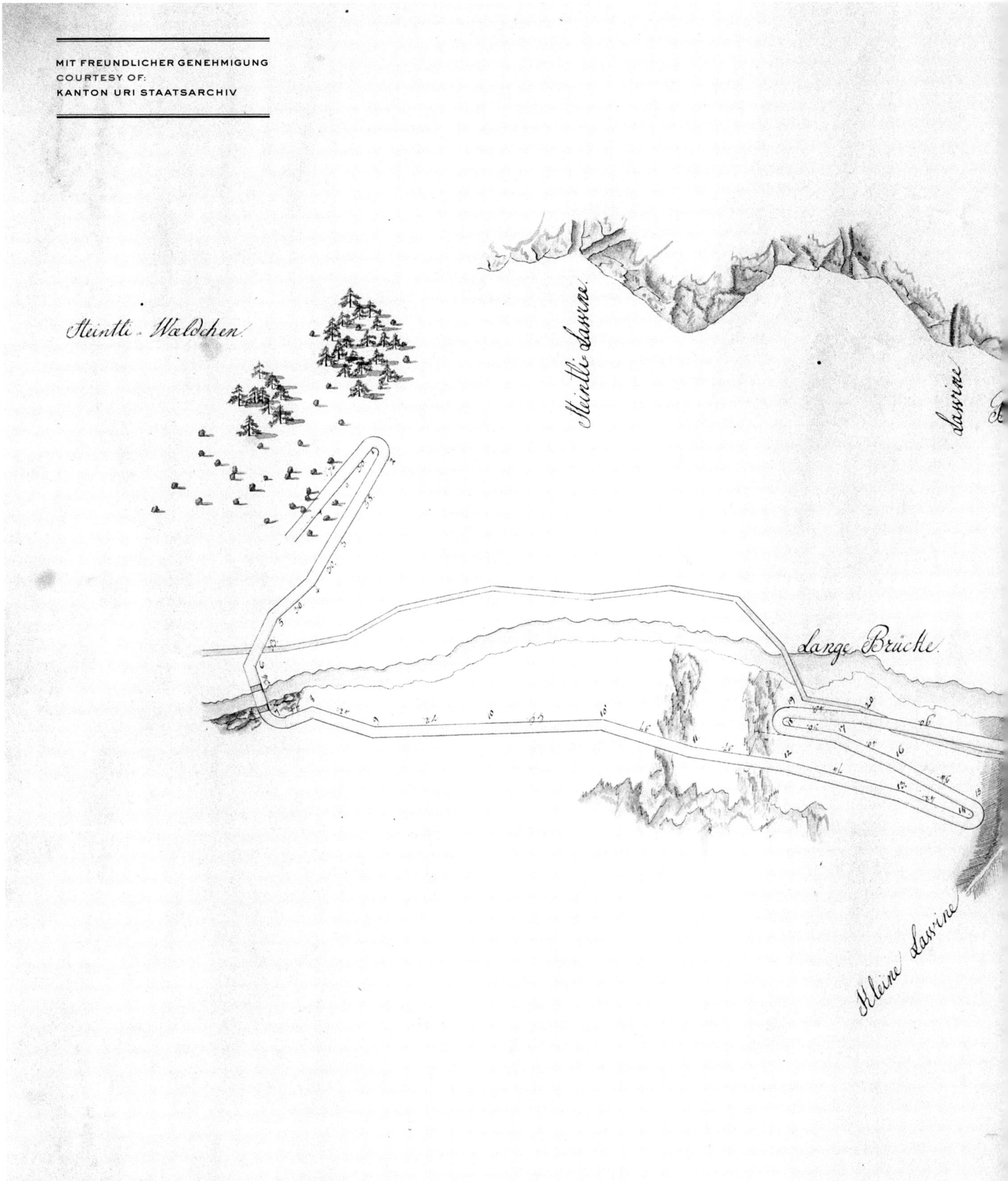
Steintli - Wäldchen
Steintli-Lawine
Lawine
Lange Brücke
Kleine Lawine

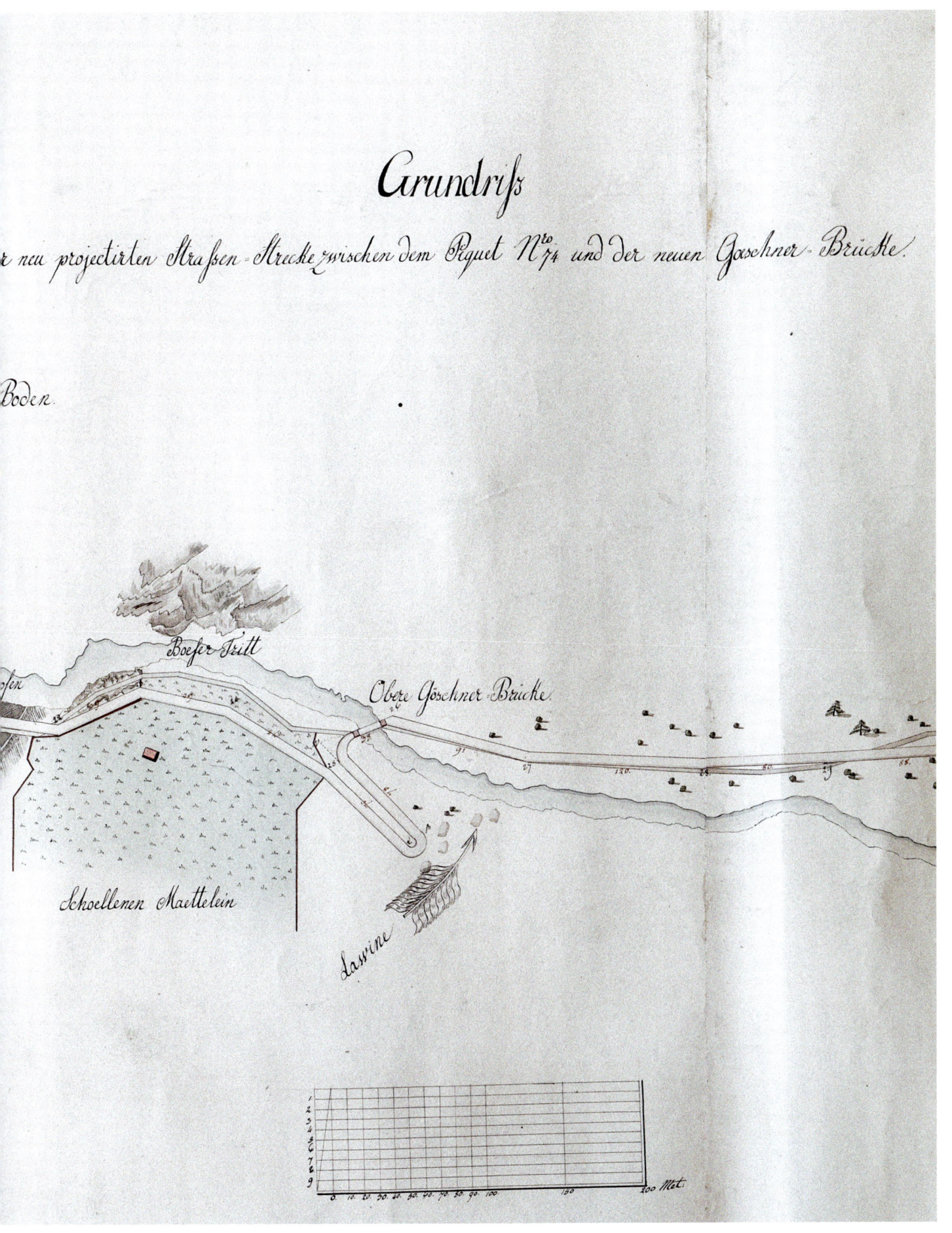

der Passhöhe verschanzt hatten. Doch Suworows Soldaten gelang es, das Hospiz einzunehmen und den Gegner erst durch das Urserental, schließlich nach erbitterten Gefechten um die teilweise zerstörte Teufelsbrücke aus der Schöllenen zurückzudrängen. In Altdorf angekommen, musste Suworow jedoch feststellen, dass der von ihm erwartete Weg entlang des Vierwaldstättersees in Richtung Schwyz nicht existierte. Bei Schneetreiben führte er seine erschöpfte Armee über den Kinzigpass ins Muotatal, wo ihn die Nachricht der Niederlage der Koalitionstruppen bei Zürich erreichte. In einer militärischen Tour de Force trat Suworows Armee über den Pragelpass und den Panixerpass den Rückzug ins Bündnerland an, von wo sich die entkräfteten Soldaten teils barfuß zurück nach Österreich flüchteten. Rund 4.000 Mann waren bei dem alpinen Gewaltmarsch ums Leben gekommen.

Trotz des französischen Sieges konnte sich die Helvetische Republik nach eskalierenden inneren Konflikten nicht lange halten. 1803 diktierte Napoleon der Schweiz seine »Mediationsverfassung«, mit der die alte föderalistische Struktur wieder hergestellt wurde – allerdings mit autonomen Kantonen. Napoleon appellierte an die Schweizer Eidgenossen, nicht nach Größe zu streben, sondern die Neutralität zu wählen, die strategisch wichtigen Alpenpässe wie den Gotthard den äußeren Einflüssen zu entziehen und somit zwischen den Großmächten Europas das Gleichgewicht zu garantieren. Nach der Niederlage Napoleons wurde die Schweiz schließlich 1815 beim Wiener Kongress vertraglich zur »immerwährenden bewaffneten Neutralität« verpflichtet. Dies akzeptieren die mittlerweile 22 Kantone noch im selben Jahr in ihrem Schweizerischen Bundesvertrag. Wilhelm Tell, der seit der Veröffentlichung von Schillers Drama als Freiheitsheld der eidgenössischen Gründungslegende an Popularität gewonnen hatte, wurde indes zur Integrationsfigur und diente dazu, im jungen Bund den inneren Zusammenhalt zu stärken. Auch das Narrativ der »Willensnation«, die aus eigenem Freiheitsdrang die Neutralität gewählt hatte, verfestigte sich im Laufe des 19. Jahrhunderts im Rückgriff auf die Legende vom Rütlischwur.

Die Gotthardstraße entsteht

Inmitten der Wirren des Krieges und der Neuordnung Europas war die verkehrstechnische Erschließung der Alpen vorangeschritten. Schon im Herbst 1805 war die von Napoleon beauftragte, 63 Kilometer lange Simplonstrasse als erste neuzeitliche Fahrstraße der Nordalpen vollendet worden. 1816 begann der Bau der Passstraßen über den Splügen, die 1822 fertiggestellt wurde. Zwischen 1818 und 1823 entstand die Straße über den San Bernardino Pass, über den schon bald die ersten Postkutschen rollten. Schon 1803 hatte der Kanton Tessin damit begonnen, die Fahrstraße von Süden unter der Leitung des Ingenieurs Francesco Domenico Meschini in Richtung Gotthard auszubauen. In Uri hatte man zunächst

see towards Schwyz did not exist. In driving snow, he led his exhausted army over the Kinzig Pass into Muota Valley, where he was informed of the defeat of the coalition troops near Zurich. In a military tour de force, Suvorov's army retreated over the Pragel and Panixer Passes into the canton of Grisons, from where the enfeebled soldiers, some of them barefoot, fled back to Austria. Around 4,000 men died in the forced march over the Alps.

Despite the French victory, the Helvetic Republic was unable to survive for long due to escalating internal conflicts. In 1803, Napoleon issued his 'Act of Mediation' to the Swiss, effectively restoring the old federalist structure, albeit with autonomous cantons. Napoleon appealed to the Swiss Confederates to temper their ambitions and opt instead for neutrality, to deprive external influences of the strategically important Alpine passes such as the Gotthard and thus guarantee the balance between the great powers of Europe. After Napoleon's defeat, a declaration was signed at the Congress of Vienna in 1815 contractually binding Switzerland to 'perpetual armed neutrality'. This was ratified by the now 22 cantons that same year in the Swiss Federal Treaty. William Tell, who had gained in popularity as a freedom fighter hero of the national founding legend since the publication of Schiller's drama, became a paragon of integration and served to strengthen the internal cohesion of the young federation. Even the narrative of the 'nation united by choice', which had chosen neutrality out of its own desire for freedom, became increasingly more stable during the 19th century in reference to the legend of the Rütli oath.

The Gotthard Road Evolves

In the midst of the turmoil of war and the restructuring of Europe, developments for traffic access through the Alps continued. As early as the autumn of 1805, the 63-kilometre-long Simplon Road, which Napoleon had commissioned, had been completed as the first modern driveable road of the northern Alps. In 1816, construction of the pass roads over the Splügen began and was finished in 1822. Between 1818 and 1823, the road over the San Bernardino Pass was developed and soon the first mail coaches rolled over it. Already in 1803, the canton of Ticino had begun extension work on the road from the south towards the Gotthard under the direction of engineer Francesco Domenico Meschini. In Uri, the high costs of making the road 'driveable' had deterred them at first, however, with the opening of the Splügen and San Bernardino links for carriage traffic, the economic existence of the Gotthard route was suddenly at stake, hence Meschini's plans for the entire road construction were accepted. After initial financing problems, the costs were shared equally between the cantons of Basel, Solothurn, Lucerne, Uri and Ticino. Between 1819 and 1824, the road between Amsteg and Göschenen was built, followed by the challenging section of the pass between Göschenen

ROUTE DE GOESCHENEN-ANDERMATT.

URNERLOCH.

LE PONT DU DIABLE.

TEUFELSBRÜCKE.

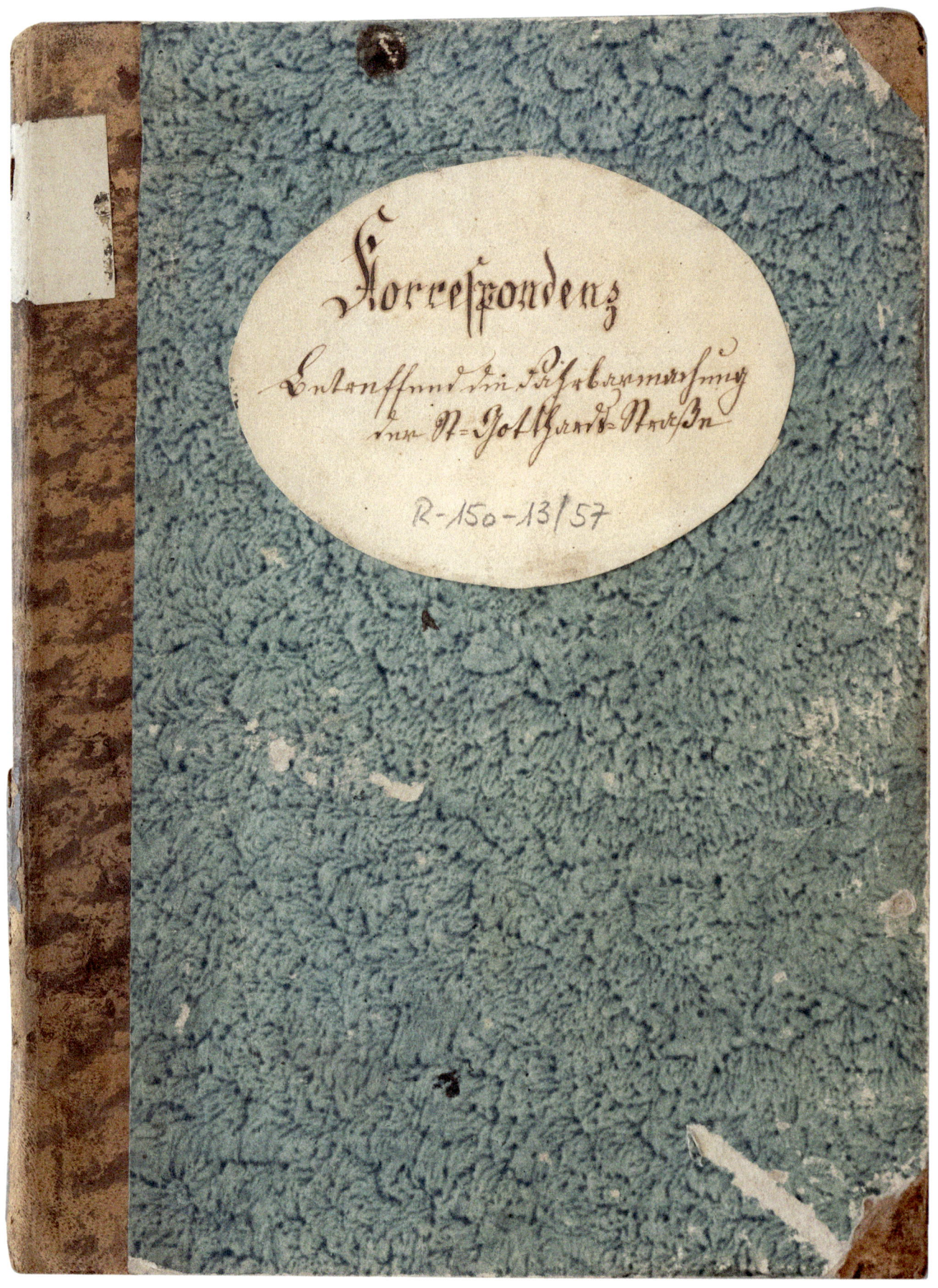

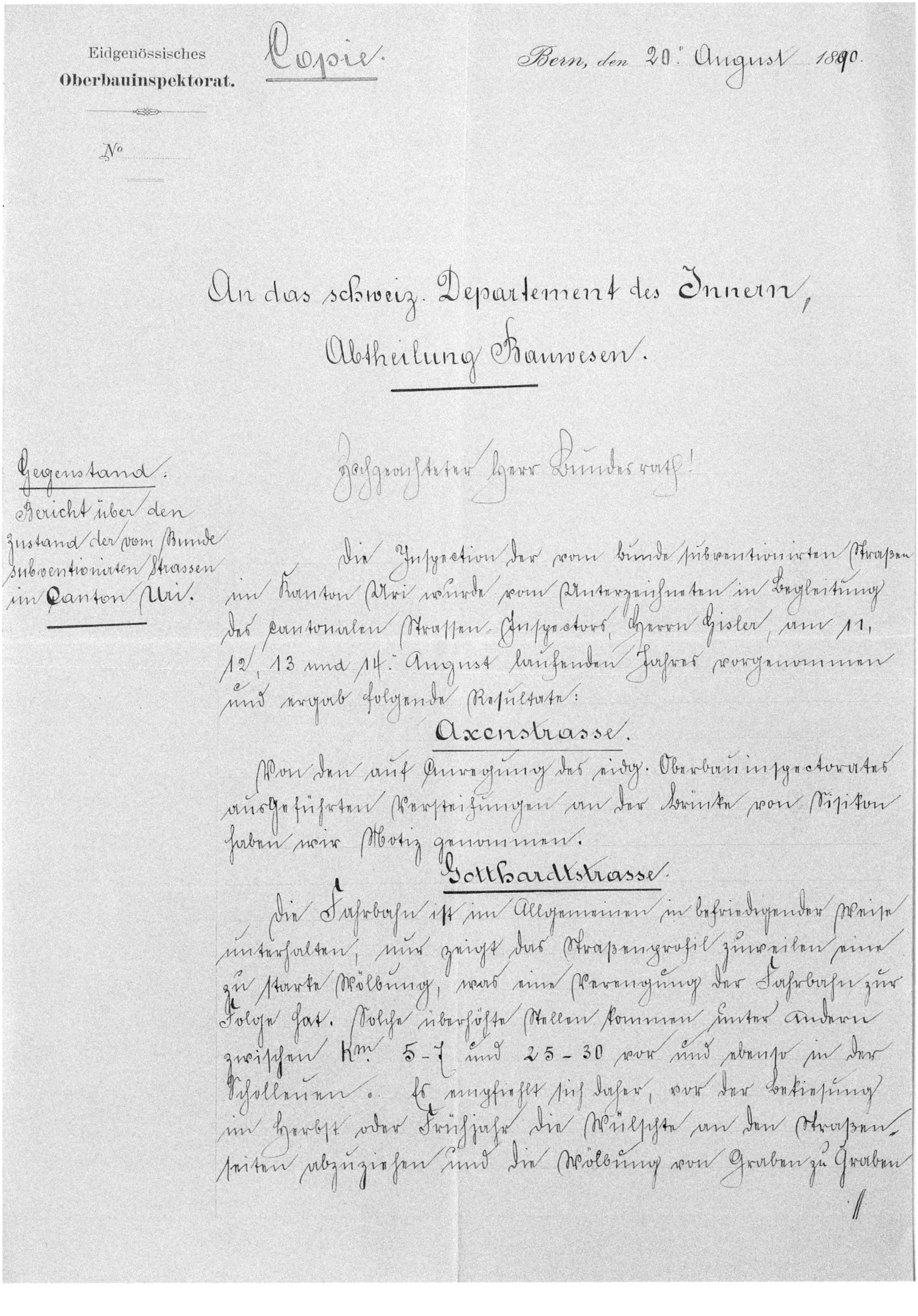

Eidgenössisches Oberbauinspektorat.

Copie.

Bern, den 20. August 1890.

N°

An das schweiz. Departement des Innern,
Abtheilung Bauwesen.

Gegenstand:
Bericht über den Zustand der vom Bunde subventionirten Strassen im Kanton Uri.

Hochgeachteter Herr Bundesrath!

Die Inspection der vom Bunde subventionirten Strassen im Kanton Uri wurde vom Unterzeichneten in Begleitung des kantonalen Strassen-Inspectors, Herrn Gisler, am 11, 12, 13 und 14. August laufenden Jahres vorgenommen und ergab folgende Resultate:

Axenstrasse.

Von den auf Anregung des eidg. Oberbauinspectorates ausgeführten Verzeichnissen an der Brücke von Sisikon haben wir Notiz genommen.

Gotthardtstrasse.

Die Fahrbahn ist im Allgemeinen in befriedigender Weise unterhalten, nur zeigt das Strassenprofil zuweilen eine zu starke Wölbung, was eine Verengung der Fahrbahn zur Folge hat. Solche überhöhte Stellen kommen unter Andern zwischen Km 5–7 und 25–30 vor und ebenso in der Schöllenen. Es empfiehlt sich daher, vor der Entziehung im Herbst oder Frühjahr die Wülste an den Strassenseiten abzuziehen und die Wölbung von Graben zu Graben

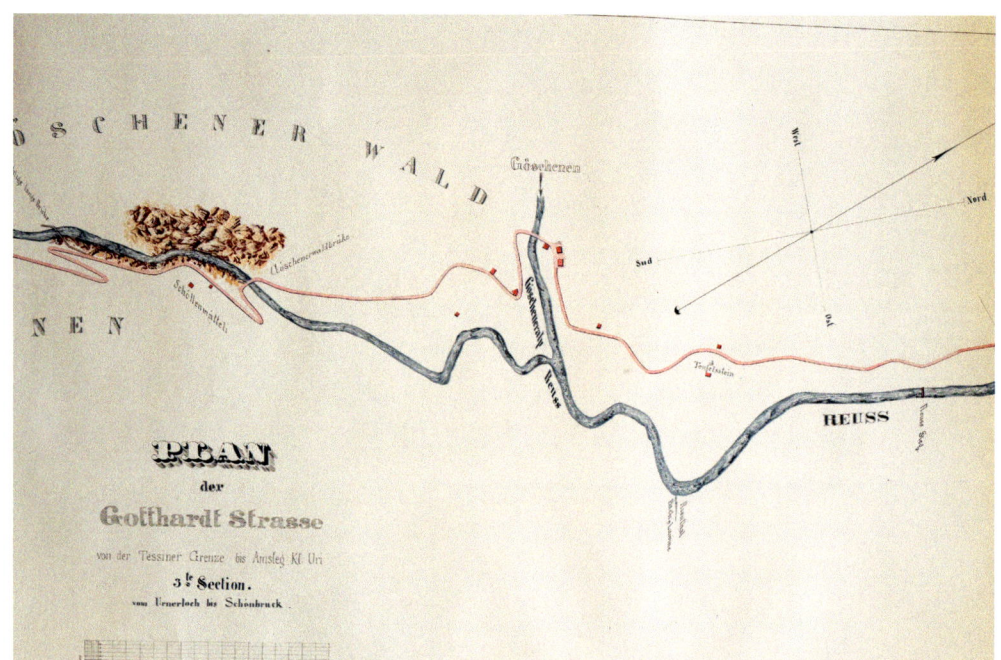

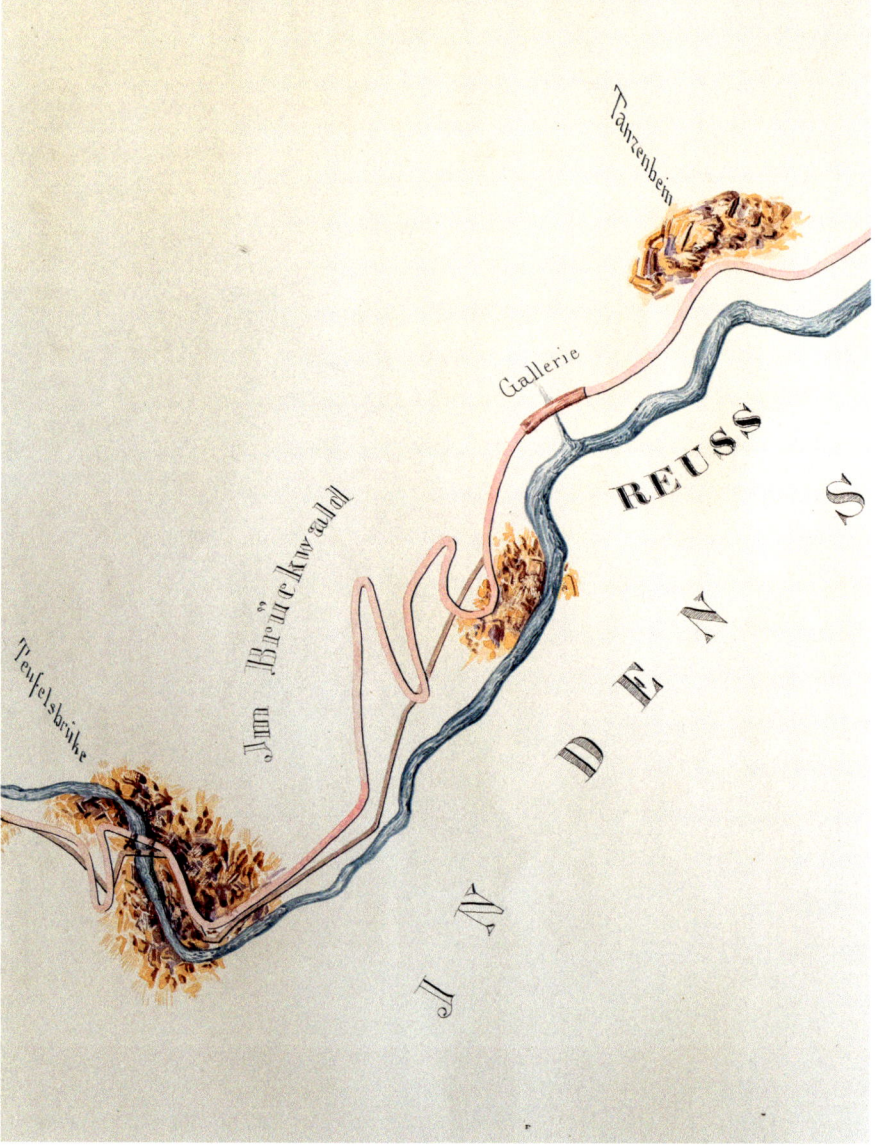

MIT FREUNDLICHER GENEHMIGUNG
COURTESY OF:
KANTON URI STAATSARCHIV
KANTON TESSIN STAATSARCHIV

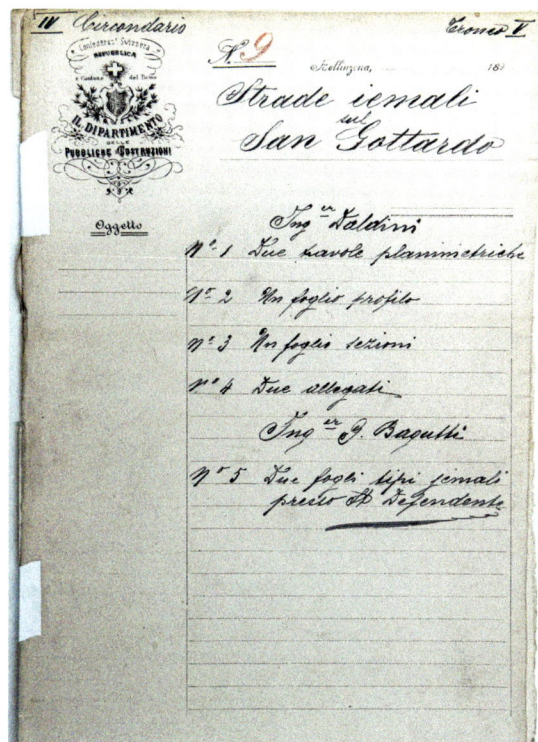
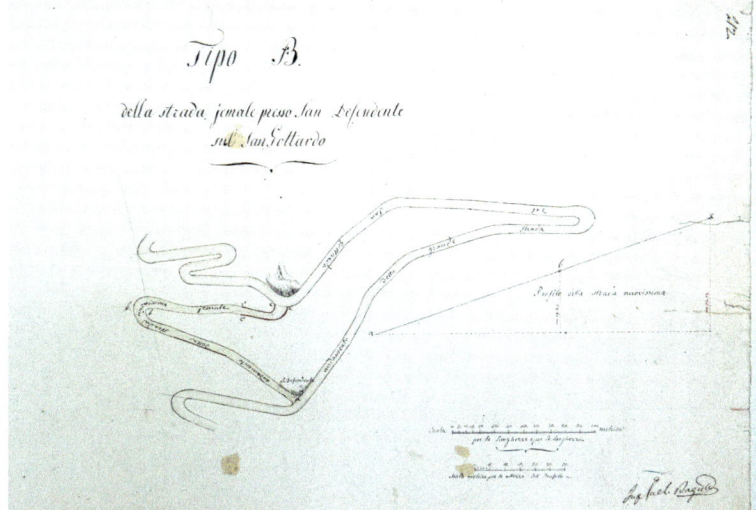
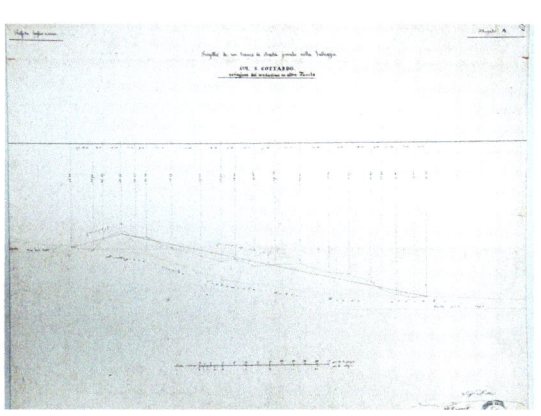
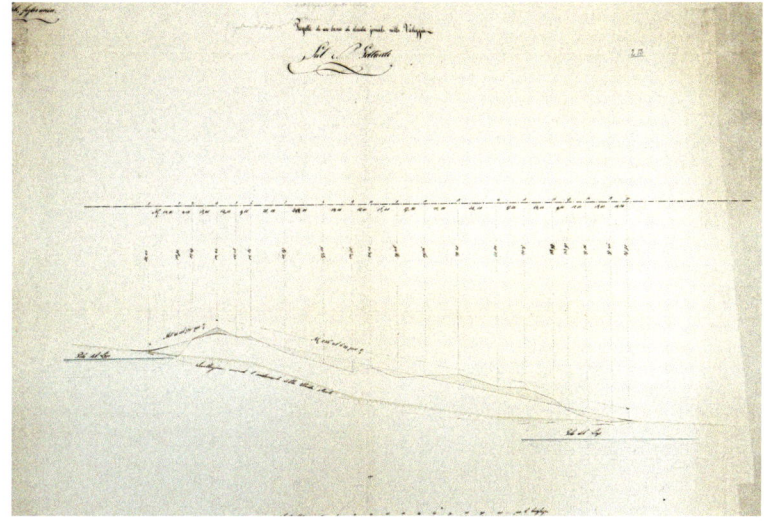

Schöllenen mit Teufelsbrücke

Gotthardstrasse - Val Tremola

GOTTHARDBAHN nörd. Seite

963 San Gottardo - Gotthardhospiz (2094 m s. m.)

Gotthard-Hospiz, Monument A. Guex

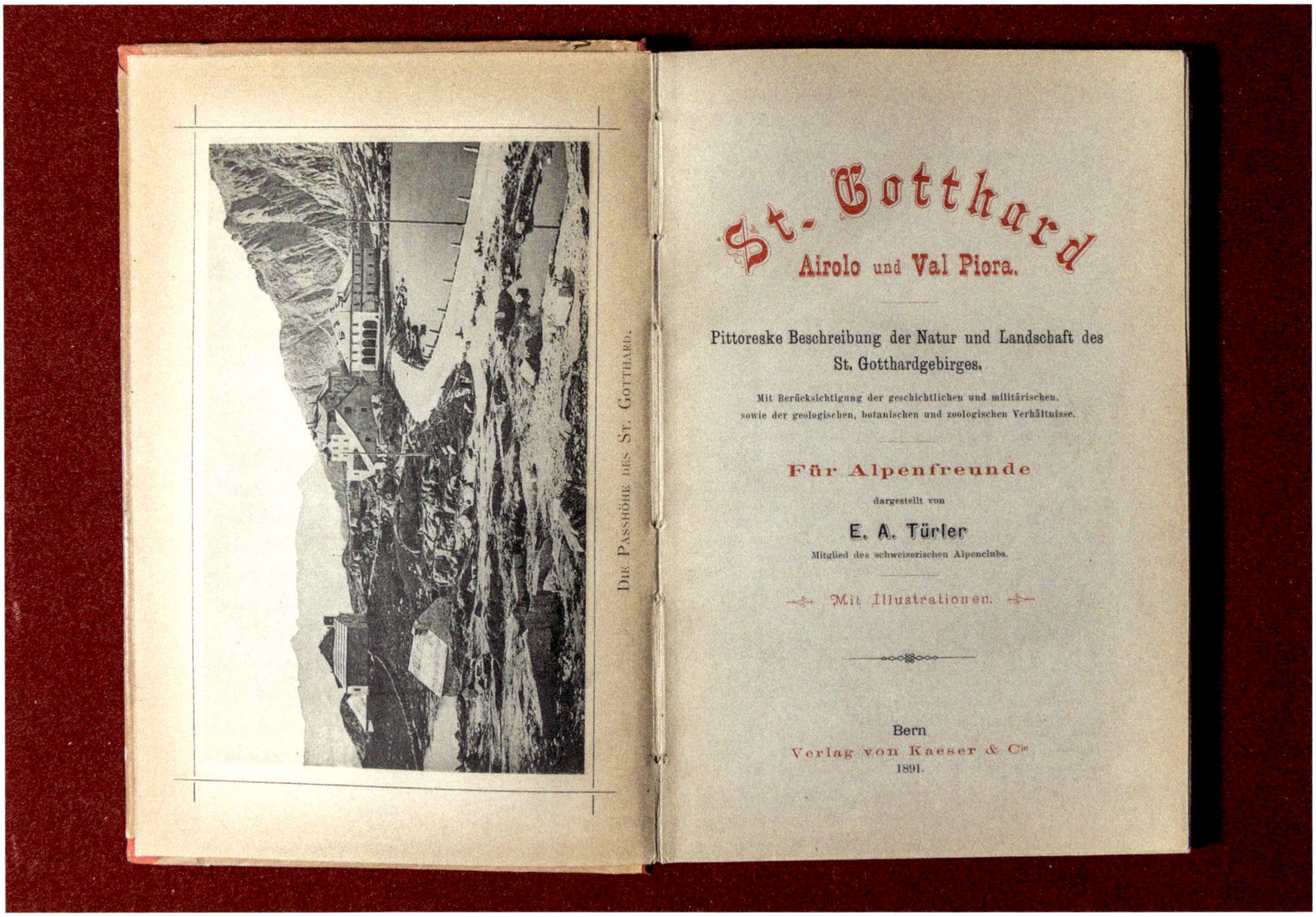

DIE PASSHÖHE DES ST. GOTTHARD.

St.-Gotthard
Airolo und Val Piora.

Pittoreske Beschreibung der Natur und Landschaft des
St. Gotthardgebirges.

Mit Berücksichtigung der geschichtlichen und militärischen,
sowie der geologischen, botanischen und zoologischen Verhältnisse.

Für Alpenfreunde
dargestellt von
E. A. Türler
Mitglied des schweizerischen Alpenclubs.

— Mit Illustrationen. —

Bern
Verlag von Kaeser & Cie
1891.

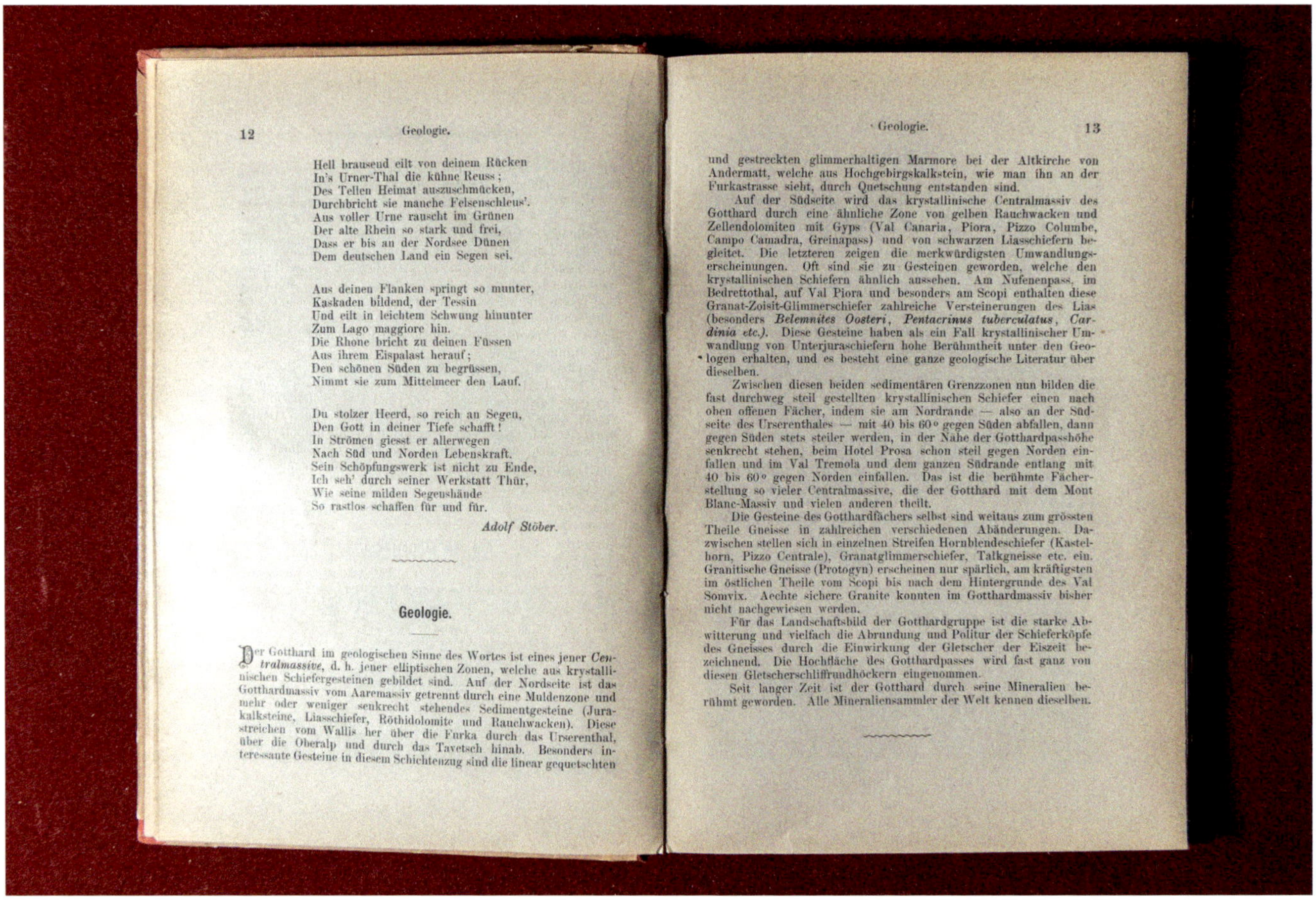

---

12   Geologie.

Hell brauseud eilt von deinem Rücken
In's Urner-Thal die kühne Reuss;
Des Tellen Heimat auszuschmücken,
Durchbricht sie manche Felsenschleus'.
Aus voller Urne rauscht im Grünen
Der alte Rhein so stark und frei,
Dass er bis an der Nordsee Dünen
Dem deutschen Land ein Segen sei.

Aus deinen Flanken springt so munter,
Kaskaden bildend, der Tessin
Und eilt in leichtem Schwung hinunter
Zum Lago maggiore hin.
Die Rhone bricht zu deinen Füssen
Aus ihrem Eispalast herauf;
Den schönen Süden zu begrüssen,
Nimmt sie zum Mittelmeer den Lauf.

Du stolzer Heerd, so reich an Segen,
Den Gott in deiner Tiefe schafft!
In Strömen giesst er allerwegen
Nach Süd und Norden Lebenskraft.
Sein Schöpfungswerk ist noch nicht zu Ende,
Ich seh' durch seiner Werkstatt Thür,
Wie seine milden Segenshände
So rastlos schaffen für und für.

Adolf Stöber.

Geologie.

Der Gotthard im geologischen Sinne des Wortes ist eines jener *Centralmassive*, d. h. jener elliptischen Zonen, welche aus krystallinischen Schiefergesteinen gebildet sind. Auf der Nordseite ist das Gotthardmassiv vom Aaremassiv getrennt durch eine Muldenzone und mehr oder weniger senkrecht stehende Sedimentgesteine (Jurakalksteine, Liasschiefer, Röthidolomite und Rauchwacken). Diese streichen vom Wallis her über die Furka durch das Urserenthal, über die Oberalp und durch das Tavetsch hinab. Besonders interessante Gesteine in diesem Schichtenzug sind die linear gequetschten

Geologie.   13

und gestreckten glimmerhaltigen Marmore bei der Altkirche von Andermatt, welche aus Hochgebirgskalkstein, wie man ihn an der Furkastrasse sieht, durch Quetschung entstanden sind.

Auf der Südseite wird das krystallinische Centralmassiv des Gotthard durch eine ähnliche Zone von gelben Rauchwacken und Zellendolomiten mit Gyps (Val Canaria, Piora, Pizzo Columbe, Campo Camadra, Greinapass) und von schwarzen Liasschiefern begleitet. Die letzteren zeigen die merkwürdigsten Umwandlungserscheinungen. Oft sind sie zu Gesteinen geworden, welche den krystallinischen Schiefern ähnlich aussehen. Am Nufenenpass, im Bedrettothal, auf Val Piora und besonders am Scopi enthalten diese Granat-Zoisit-Glimmerschiefer zahlreiche Versteinerungen des Lias (besonders *Belemnites Oosteri, Pentacrinus tuberculatus, Cardinia* etc.). Diese Gesteine haben als ein Fall krystallinischer Umwandlung von Unterjuraschiefern hohe Berühmtheit unter den Geologen erhalten, und es besteht eine ganze geologische Literatur über dieselben.

Zwischen diesen beiden sedimentären Grenzzonen nun bilden die fast durchweg steil gestellten krystallinischen Schiefer einen nach oben offenen Fächer, indem sie am Nordrande — also an der Südseite des Urserenthales — mit 40 bis 60° gegen Süden abfallen, dann gegen Süden stets steiler werden, in der Nähe der Gotthardpasshöhe senkrecht stehen, beim Hotel Prosa schon steil gegen Norden einfallen und in Val Tremola und dem ganzen Südrande entlang mit 40 bis 60° gegen Norden einfallen. Das ist die berühmte Fächerstellung so vieler Centralmassive, die der Gotthard mit dem Mont Blanc-Massiv und vielen anderen theilt.

Die Gesteine des Gotthardfächers selbst sind weitaus zum grössten Theile Gneisse in zahlreichen verschiedenen Abänderungen. Dazwischen stellen sich in einzelnen Streifen Hornblendeschiefer (Kastelhorn, Pizzo Centrale), Granatglimmerschiefer, Talkgneisse etc. ein. Granitische Gneisse (Protogyn) erscheinen nur spärlich, am kräftigsten im östlichen Theile vom Scopi bis nach dem Hintergrunde des Val Somvix. Aechte sichere Granite konnten im Gotthardmassiv bisher nicht nachgewiesen werden.

Für das Landschaftsbild der Gotthardgruppe ist die starke Abwitterung und vielfach die Abrundung und Politur der Schieferköpfe des Gneisses durch die Einwirkung der Gletscher der Eiszeit bezeichnend. Die Hochfläche des Gotthardpasses wird fast ganz von diesen Gletscherschliffrundhöckern eingenommen.

Seit langer Zeit ist der Gotthard durch seine Mineralien berühmt geworden. Alle Mineraliensammler der Welt kennen dieselben.

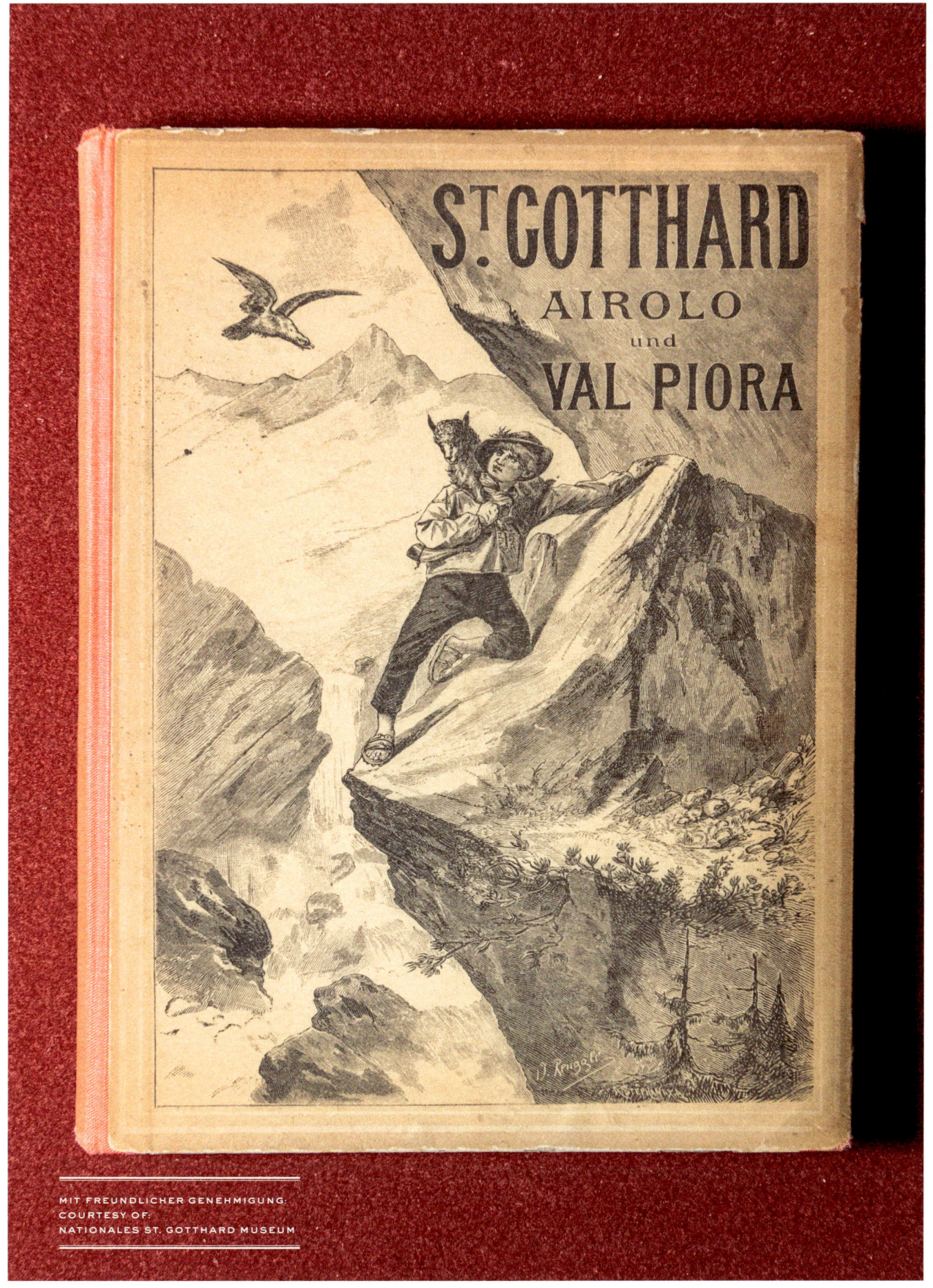

MIT FREUNDLICHER GENEHMIGUNG:
COURTESY OF:
NATIONALES ST. GOTTHARD MUSEUM

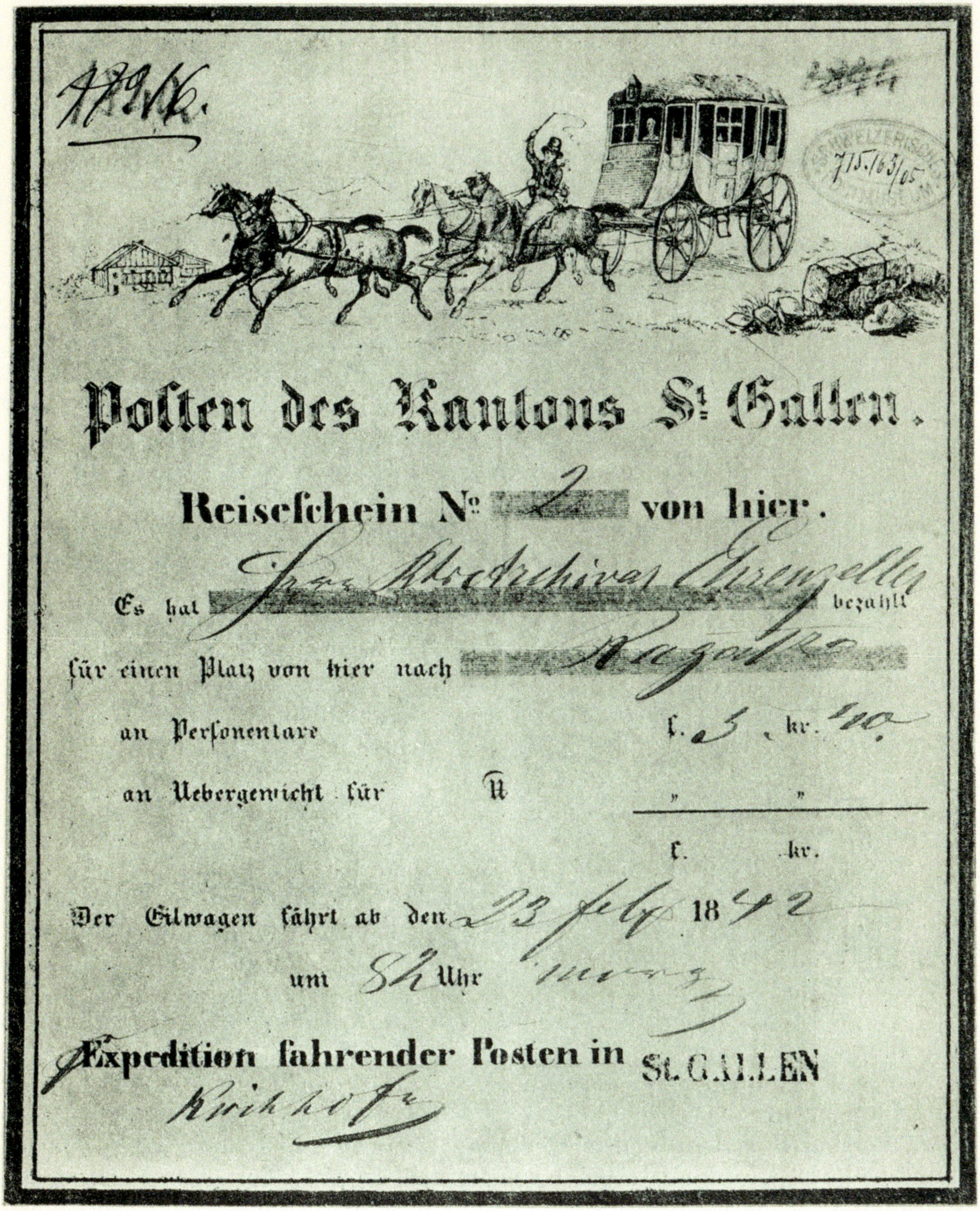

Posten des Kantons St. Gallen.

Reiseschein No. 2 von hier.

Es hat Herr Stiftsarchivar Ehrenzeller bezahlt

für einen Platz von hier nach Ragatz

an Personentaxe f. 5 . kr. 40.

an Uebergewicht für ℔ " "

f. kr.

Der Eilwagen fährt ab den 23 Febr 1842

um 8h Uhr morg.

Expedition fahrender Posten in St. GALLEN

Kirchhofer

21

noch die hohen Kosten der Fahrbarmachung gescheut – doch mit der Eröffnung der Splügen- und San-Bernardino-Verbindungen für den Wagenverkehr stand plötzlich die wirtschaftliche Existenz der Gotthardroute auf dem Spiel, und man ließ sich auf die Pläne Meschinis für den gesamten Straßenbau ein. Die Kosten wurden nach anfänglichen Finanzierungsproblemen von den Kantonen Basel, Solothurn, Luzern, Uri und Tessin gemeinsam getragen.

Zwischen 1819 und 1824 wurde die Straße zwischen Amsteg und Göschenen gebaut, von 1828 bis 1830 folgte die anspruchsvolle Passstrecke zwischen Göschenen und Airolo. Für den Bau der Serpentinenstraße durch die steile und gefährliche Tremolaschlucht wurde der Tessiner Ingenieur Francesco Meschini beauftragt. Mit 24 Spitzkehren, bis zu acht Meter hohen Kurvenmauern und gerade einmal sechs Prozent Steigung bezwang die Tremolastraße auf 4,5 Kilometern Länge ganze 341 Höhenmeter, bevor sie unterhalb des Hospizes die Passhöhe erreichte. Die Tremola wurde zum Wahrzeichen des Gotthardpasses und ist bis heute als historischer Streckenabschnitt befahrbar. Auf der Nordseite des Passes durfte der 24-jährige, vielseitig talentierte Urner Bauingenieur Karl Emanuel Müller sein Können unter Beweis stellen. Ihm gelang in der Schöllenenschlucht mit der zweiten Teufelsbrücke und ihrer Zufahrt entlang der senkrechten, 200 Meter in den Himmel ragenden Teufelswand eine architektonische Meisterleistung. Den anspruchsvollen Bau der Straße von Hospental bis zur Kantonsgrenze von Uri leitete der Ingenieur Carlo Colombara.

Der Postillon vom Gotthard

Ende des Jahres 1830 war die Gotthardstraße schließlich durchgehend für Fuhrwerke befahrbar. Die Schotterstraße war zwischen 5,5 und 7,5 Meter breit, die Steigung lag zwischen sechs und zehn Prozent. Ab 1831 wurde am Gotthard der Post- und Personentransport mit Pferdekutschen aufgenommen. Für den Handel hatte die neue Straße enorme Vorteile: Hatte ein Saumtier bloß 150 Kilo tragen können, konnte man eine vierrädrige Kutsche pro Zugpferd mit rund 500 Kilo Waren beladen. Auf besonders steilen Wegstücken musste man allerdings zusätzliche Pferde vorspannen. Für die Urner und Tessiner Saumhändler, die in den 600 Jahre nach der Öffnung der Schöllenenschlucht ein komplexes Transportwesen und Wirtschaftssystem entwickelt hatten, bedeutete der Bau der Fahrstraße allerdings das Ende ihres etablierten Geschäftsmodells. Doch die Gotthardstraße eröffnete auch neue Erwerbsmöglichkeiten. Ab 1835 verkehrten die ersten Urner Postkutschen zwischen Chiasso und Flüelen. 1837 wurde am Pass ein Post- und Zollgebäude mit Ställen und Unterkünften eingerichtet. Zudem fuhren nun Dampfschiffe auf dem Vierwaldstättersee – statt der zwölf Stunden, die man an Bord einer Ruderbarke von Luzern nach Flüelen benötigt hatte, dauerte die Überfahrt bloß noch zwei Stunden und 45 Minuten. Ab 1842

and Airolo from 1828 to 1830. For the construction of the zigzagging road through the steep and dangerous Tremola Gorge, the Ticino engineer Francesco Meschini was commissioned. Featuring 24 switchbacks, up to eight-metre-high curved walls and a gradient of just six percent, the Tremola Road overcame an elevation difference of 341 metres over 4.5 kilometres before reaching the pass summit just below the hospice. The Tremola became the landmark of the Gotthard Pass and the historic section of the route is still driveable today. On the northern side of the pass, the 24-year-old, multi-talented Uri civil engineer Karl Emanuel Müller was able to demonstrate his skills. He succeeded in creating an architectural masterpiece in the Schöllenen Gorge with the second Devil's Bridge and its approach along the 200-metre sheer vertical devil's wall. The demanding construction of the road from Hospental to the border of the Uri canton was overseen by the engineer Carlo Colombara.

The Postilion of the Gotthard

By the end of 1830, carts could finally traverse the Gotthard. The gravel road measured between 5.5 and 7.5 metres in width, with the gradient between six and ten percent. From 1831, horse-drawn coaches carried mail and passengers over the Gotthard. The route proved enormously beneficial for trade: while a pack animal could carry only 150 kilograms, the four-wheeled coaches could cope with a load weighing around 500 kilograms per horse. On particularly steep parts, however, one had to harness additional draught horses. For the muleteers from Uri and Ticino, who had developed sophisticated transport and economic systems for 600 years after the opening of the Schöllenen Gorge, the construction of the road signalled an end to their long-established business model. The Gotthard Road, however, also opened up new income opportunities. From 1835, the first Uri postal stagecoach ran a service between Chiasso and Flüelen. In 1837, a post office and customs building with stables and accommodation was set up on the pass. Moreover, steamships now plied Lake Lucerne – and instead of 12 hours, the crossing now took only two hours and 45 minutes. From 1842, the five-horse eight-seater stagecoach ran daily in both directions for fast passenger transport. In winter, the pass was also kept open by snow-shovelling roadmen and mail was carried by sled.

After the defeat of the conservation Catholic cantons in the Sonderbund Wars, in 1848 Switzerland converted to a modern federal state with a liberal constitution. From 1849, the Swiss Post replaced the cantonal and privately-run postal services. With the yellow postal stagecoaches, which now operated between the most important cities in Switzerland and soon also traversed the Alps, a new era began on the Gotthard. The so-called 'Milan route' offered space for ten people and left Flüelen at 8am, arriving at the Gotthard hospice at 4pm, travelling through Bellinzona at around 11pm to

fuhren die fünfspänniger Achtplätzerwagen für eiligen Personenverkehr sogar täglich in beide Richtungen. Im Winter wurde der Pass von Schaufelknechten offen gehalten, es verkehrten Postschlitten.

Nach der Niederlage der konservativ-katholischen Kantone in den Sonderbundkriegen wurde die Schweiz 1848 in einen modernen Bundesstaat mit liberaler Verfassung umgewandelt. Ab 1849 löste die Schweizer Post die kantonalen und privaten Postunternehmen ab. Mit den gelben Postkutschen, die fortan die wichtigsten Städte der Schweiz verbanden und auch schon bald über die Alpen verkehrten, begann auch am Gotthard eine neue Zeitrechnung. Der »Mailänderkurs« bot Platz für zehn Personen und fuhr jeweils um acht Uhr morgens in Flüelen los, erreichte um kurz nach 16 Uhr das Gotthardhospiz, passierte gegen 23 Uhr Bellinzona und traf um sieben Uhr morgens in Camerlata südlich von Como ein, von wo man in die Bahn nach Mailand umsteigen konnte. In den 23 Stunden, die man als Reisender auf dem schaukelnden und ungefederten Gefährt überdauern musste, wurden zwölf Mal die Pferde gewechselt. Während der Postillon im Dienst des Pferdehalters stand und nur einen Streckenabschnitt begleitete, blieb der Kondukteur als Postangestellter über größere Distanzen an Bord. Der Fahrpreis für die gesamte, mehr als 49 Stunden lange Reise per Postkutsche, Dampfschiff und Eisenbahn von Basel nach Mailand lag inklusive Rückfahrbillet bei stolzen 68,60 Franken – dem dreifachen Monatslohn eines Postangestellten.

Dabei konnte die Bergreise auch zu Zeiten des Postverkehrs schnell zum Albtraum werden: Kutschen wurden von Straßenräubern überfallen, Kondukteure erschossen oder von Lawinen erschlagen, ganze Reisegruppen von Schnee- und Schlammlawinen in die Tiefe gerissen. An vielen gefährlichen Stellen fehlten Schutzbauten. Im Winter konnten heftige Schneestürme den Straßenverlauf binnen Minuten unkenntlich machen. Die Pferde- und Ochsenschlitten wurden von Männern mit Schaufeln begleitet, die vorauseilten und die verschneiten Wege ebneten. Reisende und Gepäck wurden in dicke Federbetten gezurrt, die nicht nur wärmen, sondern bei möglichen Unfällen auch für Schutz sorgen sollten. Trotz des Winterdienstes blieb der Gotthardpass zwischen Oktober und April oft tagelang unpassierbar, Reisende mussten dann in den Gasthäusern, Hospizen oder dem 1866 an der Passhöhe gebauten Hotel Monte Prosa ausharren und auf besseres Wetter hoffen.

Derweil schritt der Ausbau der Zufahrten zum Sankt Gotthard rasant voran. Im Jahr 1847 wurde im Tessin der Damm zwischen Melide und Bissone eröffnet. Zwischen 1862 und 1865 bauten Uri und Schwyz entlang des Steilufers des Urnersees die Axenstraße aus und schufen damit erstmals eine für Kutschen befahrbare Landverbindung nach Norden. Somit war der Gotthard endgültig an das Verkehrsnetz der Schweiz angeschlossen. Mit

arrive in Camerlata south of Como at 7am, in time for the passengers to catch the train to Milan. Over the 23 hours, during which passengers had to endure a rocking coach without any form of suspension, the horses were changed twelve times. While the postilion worked for the horse owner and accompanied the coach on just part of the route, the conductor remained on board over the entire distance as a postal worker. The fare for the 49-hour journey by stagecoach, steamship and railroad from Basel to Milan, including a return ticket, was a staggering 68.60 Swiss francs – three times the monthly salary of a postal worker.

Nevertheless, even in the times of the early postal services, travelling over the mountains could quickly turn into a nightmare: carriages were ambushed by bandits, conductors were shot or buried by avalanches, entire tour groups were swept into the abyss by snow and mudslides. Many treacherous, hazardous places lacked protective barriers. In winter, severe snowstorms could obscure the ruts in the road within minutes. Horse and ox sleds were accompanied by men with shovels, who hurried ahead to clear the snow-covered tracks. Travellers and luggage were lashed down in thick feather quilts which kept them warm and safe in the event of an accident. Despite the winter maintenance service, the Gotthard Pass often proved impassable for days at a time between October and April, with wayfarers forced to hunker down in the inns, hospices or the Hotel Monte Prosa – built in 1866 at the pass – and wait for the weather to clear.

Meanwhile, the expansion of the roads to Saint Gotthard progressed rapidly. In 1847, the dam in Ticino between Melide and Bissone was opened. Between 1862 and 1865, Uri and Schwyz extended the Axenstraße along the steep bank of the Urner Lake, and thus created the first road link for carriages to the north. With this, the Gotthard was finally connected to the transport network of Switzerland. With the Oberalp and Furka routes, the road network in the Ursern Valley was opened up for vehicles in the 1860s. In 1849, around 14,000 people travelled on the Gotthard post coach; by 1875, the number of passengers had increased to over 72,000. The yellow coach – as portrayed in Rudolf Koller's famous but highly idealised painting Die Gotthardpost – which careens through the corners of the Tremola, became a symbol of Swiss progress.

The Construction of the Gotthard Railway

As rapidly as the popularity of mail coaches on the Gotthard grew, the decline of those glory days was just as fast. Throughout Europe, the railroad had begun its triumphal progress as a new mode of transport, and steam trains had also been gaining ground throughout Switzerland since the 1840s. The Railway Act of 1852 cleared the way for the construction of a Swiss railway net-

der Oberalpstraße und der Furkastraße wurden in den 1860er-Jahren auch die Querverbindungen im Urserental für den Fahrbetrieb erschlossen. Waren um 1849 noch rund 14.000 Reisende pro Jahr mit der Gotthardpost gereist, zählte man 1875 bereits mehr als 72.000 Passagiere. Die gelbe Kutsche, die – wie auf Rudolf Kollers berühmtem, aber stark idealisiertem Gemälde »Die Gotthardpost« – im Eiltempo durch die Kurven der Tremola brauste, war zum Symbol des Schweizerischen Fortschritts geworden.

Der Bau der Gotthardbahn

So rasant der Aufstieg der Postkutschen am Gotthard gewesen war, so schnell war ihre Ruhmeszeit aber auch schon wieder vorbei. In ganz Europa hatte die Eisenbahn als neues Transportmittel ihren Siegeszug angetreten, und auch in der Schweiz hielten die Dampfloks seit den 1840er-Jahren Einzug. Mit dem Eisenbahngesetz von 1852 war der Weg frei für den Bau eines gesamtschweizerischen Schienennetzes, wobei den Kantonen und privaten Unternehmen die Führung überlassen wurde. Nachdem 1854 in Österreich die Semmeringbahn eröffnet hatte, wurde auch die Bauplanung der neuen Gebirgsbahnen am Brenner und Mont Cenis konkret. Unter dem Druck der Konkurrenz diskutierten Ingenieure, Politiker und Wirtschaftsführer in der Schweiz den Bau einer Eisenbahnstrecke über und durch das Gotthardmassiv. Einer der einflussreichsten und stimmgewaltigsten Fürsprecher des ambitionierten Projektes war der Zürcher Staatsmann, Unternehmer und Eisenbahnförderer Alfred Escher, der bereits die Nordostbahn betrieb. Waren zunächst noch Alternativstrecken über den Lukmanier- und Grimselpass als alpine Transitrouten im Gespräch, konnten die Gotthardkantone schließlich ihren Alpenpass als schnellste und kürzeste Verbindung durchsetzen. 1869 erhielt das Bauvorhaben grünes Licht, 1871 wurde die Finanzierung der Gotthardbahn gesichert und eine substantielle Beteiligung des deutschen Reiches und des Königreichs Italien per Staatsvertrag vereinbart.

Der Plan war verwegen und architektonisch höchst anspruchsvoll: Auf der 205 Kilometer langen Strecke zwischen Immensee und Chiasso, die fast zur Hälfte durch schroffes Gebirge führte, sollten 108 Brücken und 60 Tunnels entstehen. Im Norden mussten 634 Höhenmeter überwunden werden, im Süden waren es sogar 849 Höhenmeter. Die maximale Steigung durfte allerdings nicht mehr als 28 Promille betragen, der Kurvenradius derweil nicht 300 Meter unterschreiten. Im Reusstal und in der Leventina mussten deshalb lange Steigungsrampen und gewaltige Kehrtunnels angelegt werden. An besonders gefährdeten Hängen waren zum Schutz der Strecke zudem Lawinenriegel notwendig. Das eigentliche Herzstück der neuen Gotthardbahn war jedoch ein 14,9 Kilometer langer Tunnel zwischen Göschenen und Airolo. Die Bauleitung wurde dem Ingenieur und Unternehmer Louis Favre übertragen, der vertraglich zugesichert

---

> **Der Plan war verwegen und architektonisch höchst anspruchsvoll: Auf der 205 Kilometer langen Strecke zwischen Immensee und Chiasso, die fast zur Hälfte durch schroffes Gebirge führte, sollten 108 Brücken und 60 Tunnels entstehen.**

> **The plan was daring and architecturally very ambitious: over the 205-kilometre route between Immensee and Chiasso, half of which went through rugged mountains, 108 bridges and 60 tunnels were needed.**

work, with the cantons and private companies taking charge. After the opening of the Semmering Railway in Austria in 1854, construction plans for new trans-Alpine railway lines over the Brenner and Mont Cenis gained traction. Coming under pressure from the competition, engineers, politicians and captains of industry in Switzerland discussed the construction of a railway across and through the Gotthard massif. One of the most influential and vociferous advocates of this ambitious project was the Zurich statesman, entrepreneur and railway sponsor, Alfred Escher, who already ran the Swiss Northeastern Railway (Nordostbahn NOB). Although alternative routes via the Lukmanier and Grimsel passes were initially considered as Alpine transit lines, the Gotthard cantons finally managed to convince others that their Alpine pass was the fastest and shortest connection. In 1869, the construction project got the green light. In 1871, the financing of the Gotthard Railway was secured, with the German Reich and the Kingdom of Italy contributing significantly to the railway construction as agreed per state treaties.

The plan was daring and architecturally very ambitious: over the 205-kilometre route between Immensee and Chiasso, half of which went through rugged mountains, 108 bridges and 60 tunnels were needed. To the north, an elevation difference of 634 metres had to be overcome; in the south the elevation gain was as much as 849 metres. The maximum gradient, however, could not exceed 28/1000; the corner radius could be no less than 300 metres. In the Reuss Valley and the Leventina, long ascent ramps and massive spiralling tunnels had to be creat-

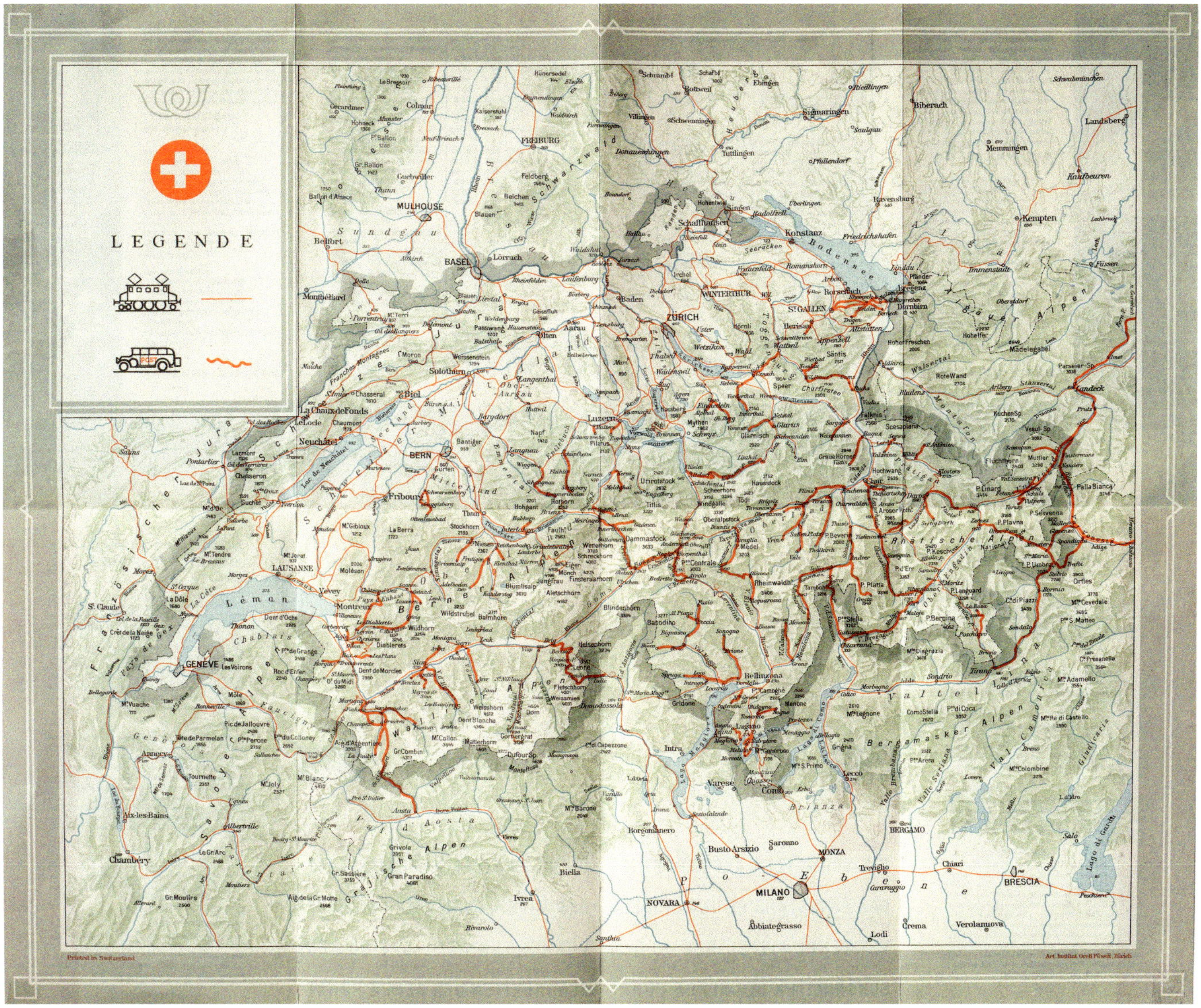

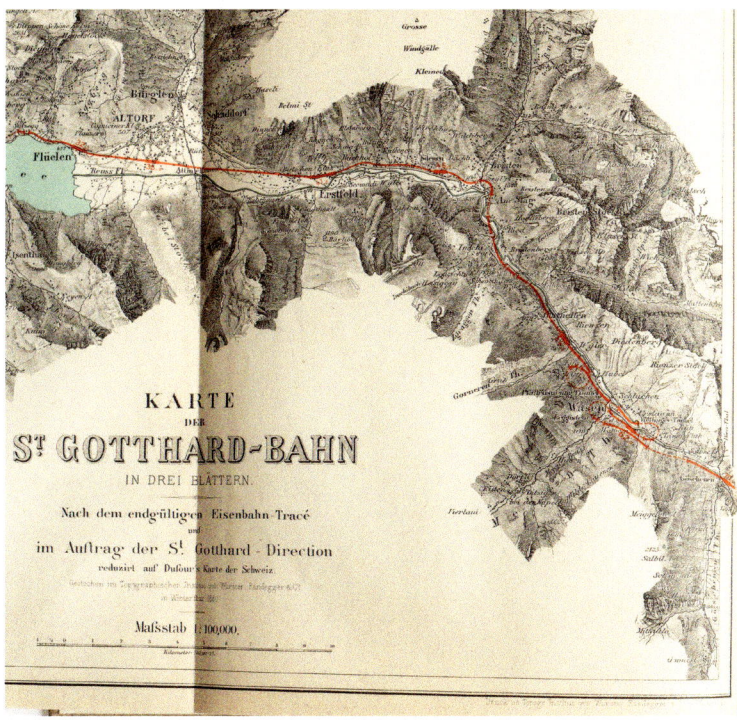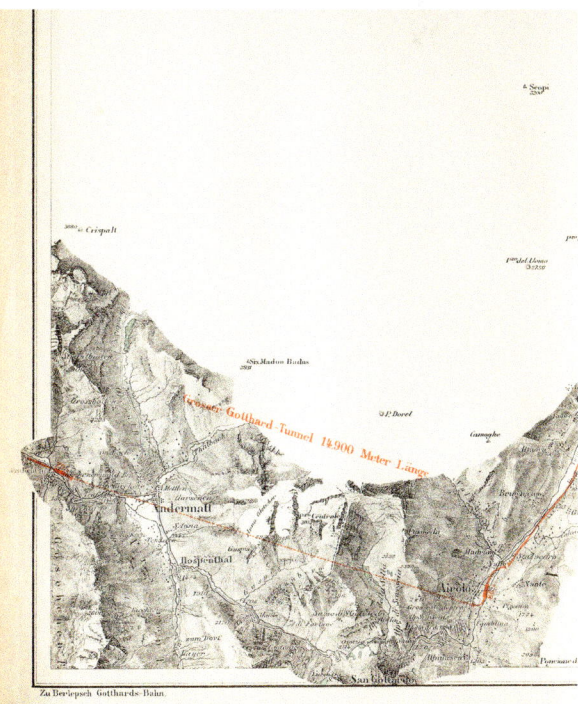

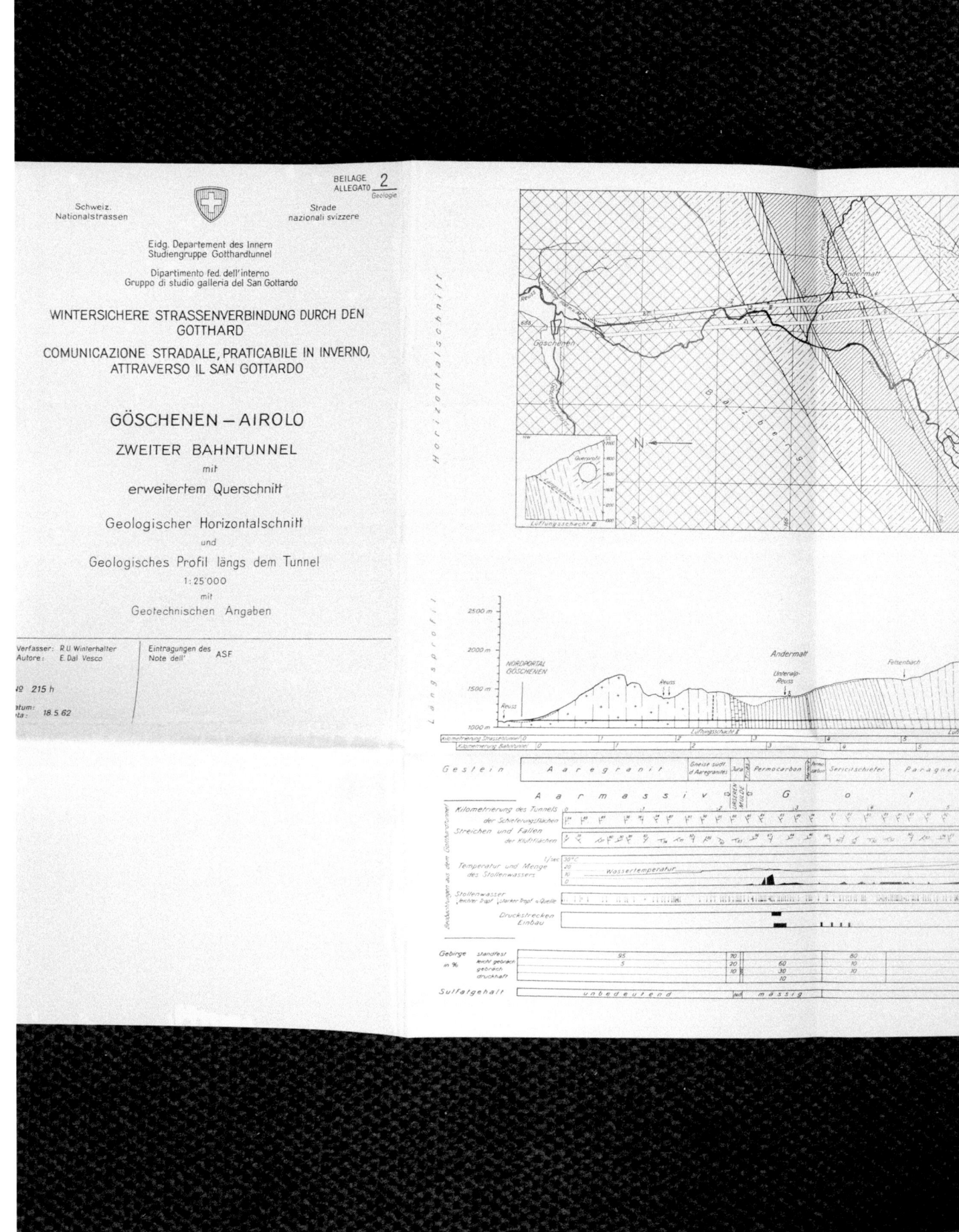

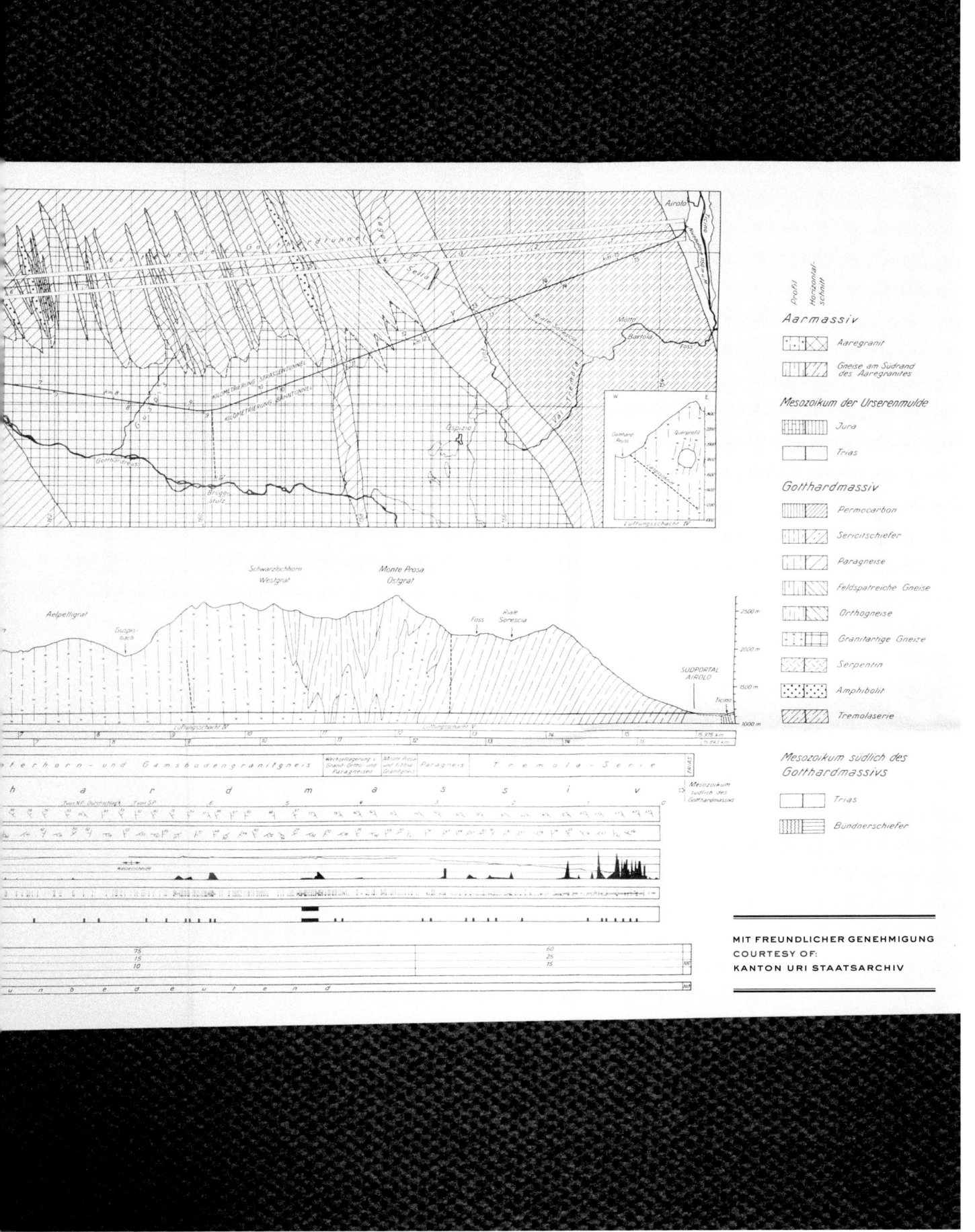

hatte, die Teilstrecke in nur acht Jahren und zu einem Preis von 56 Millionen Franken fertigzustellen – und bei Verzögerungen empfindliche Strafzahlungen zu leisten. Im Herbst 1872 begannen die Arbeiten am Tunnel, doch schon bald traten die ersten Schwierigkeiten auf. Favre hatte die geologische Komplexität des Gotthardmassivs unterschätzt, immer wieder kam es zu Verzögerungen. Durchschnittlich waren an den Tunnelbaustellen in Göschenen und Airolo rund 2.600 Arbeiter im Einsatz, die sich bei unerträglicher Hitze, schlechter Luft und meist bis zu den Knien im Wasser stehend durch den Stein kämpften. Die Sicherheitsvorkehrungen waren gering, immer wieder kam es zu tödlichen Unfällen, Krankheiten gingen um. 1875 kam es schließlich zum Streik, bei dem vier Arbeiter erschossen wurden.

1876 musste Alfred Escher bekannt geben, dass der Bau der Gotthardbahn nicht wie geplant 187 Millionen, sondern rund 290 Millionen Franken kosten würde. Escher und sein Oberingenieur Robert Gerwig traten zurück, Louis Favre drohte die Insolvenz, der Bund sprang zur Subventionierung der Mehrkosten ein, auch Italien und Deutschland mussten erneut in die Taschen greifen. Am 29. Februar 1880 vermeldeten die Ingenieure schließlich den Durchstich: Durch den Gotthard führte nun der längste Tunnel der Welt. Sein Baumeister Louis Favre erlebte den historischen Moment nicht mehr – er war im Juli 1879 bei einer Begehung im Tunnel an einem Riss in der Bauch-Aorta verstorben.

Während im Berg unter Hochdruck an der Fertigstellung des Bahntunnels gearbeitet wurde, ging auf dem Gotthard nach nur 50 Jahren die glorreiche Epoche der Postkutschen zu Ende: Am 31. Dezember 1881 erfolgte die letzte Postübergabe am Gotthardhospiz. Alois Zgraggen – ener »letzte Postillon«, der die Gotthardpost gut zwei Jahrzehnte begleitet hatte und bei der Abschiedsfahrt von Flüelen nach Mailand auf der Kutsche saß – wurde zur schweizerischen Legende. Die Postkutsche selbst ist bis heute im Schweizerischen Landesmuseum zu sehen.

Nach mehr als 600 Jahren, in denen sich der Fernverkehr auf dem Gotthardpass stets verdichtet und beschleunigt hatte, kehrte auf den staubigen Serpentinen zwischen Göschenen und Airolo plötzlich Ruhe ein. Tief unten im Berg wurde derweil das nächste Kapitel in der Fortschrittsgeschichte des Gotthards geschrieben: Anfang das Jahres 1882 rollten die ersten Postzüge durch den neuen Tunnel, im Mai fanden in Luzern und Mailand die großen Feierlichkeiten zur Eröffnung statt. »Die Scheidewand, welche die Nationen trennte, ist gefallen«, sprach Bundespräsident Simeon Bavier. »Die Länder sind einander näher gerückt und dem Weltverkehr geöffnet.« Alfred Escher, der in Ungnade gefallene Bahnpionier und Bezwinger des großen Sankt Gotthard, war bei der Eröffnung aus Krankheitsgründen nicht anwesend. Am 1. Juni 1882 nahm die Gotthardbahn schließlich zwischen Immensee und Chiasso ihren fahrplanmäßi-

ed. On particularly hazardous slopes, avalanche barriers were necessary to protect the railway line.

The true masterstroke of the new Gotthard Railway, however, was a 14.9-kilometre-long tunnel between Göschenen and Airolo. Management of the construction was entrusted to the engineer and businessman, Louis Favre, who had agreed by contract to complete the stage in just eight years at a cost of 56 million francs – and to pay stiff penalties for any delays. In autumn 1872, no sooner had work began on the tunnel than the first difficulties arose. Favre had underestimated the geological complexity of the Gotthard massif, and this caused delays. On average, around 2,600 workers toiled at the tunnel construction sites at Göschenen and Airolo, battling their way through the rock in unbearable heat, bad air and often standing up to their knees in water. There were very few safety measures, and fatal accidents and illness took many lives.

In 1875, a strike broke out and four workers were shot dead. In 1876, Alfred Escher had to disclose that the construction of the Gotthard Railway would not cost the planned 187 million francs, but more in the realm of 290 million francs. Escher and his chief engineer Robert Gerwig resigned, Louis Favre was facing bankruptcy, and the federal government intervened to subsidise the additional costs, with Italy and Germany again having to dig into their own pockets. On 29 February 1880, the engineers finally announced the breakthrough: the tunnel through the Gotthard was now the longest in the world. Alas, its architect Louis Favre did not witness this historic moment – in July 1879 while inspecting the tunnel he died of a ruptured abdominal aorta.

While work continued at high pace on the completion of the railway tunnel through the mountain, the glorious stagecoach era gradually ground to a halt after just 50 years: on 31 December 1881, the last mail delivery was handed over at the Gotthard hospice. Alois Zgraggen – the 'last postilion', who had accompanied the Gotthard mail for a good two decades and sat on the coach during its final farewell journey from Flüelen to Milan – became a Swiss legend. The stagecoach itself can still be seen in the Swiss National Museum.

After more than 600 years, during which time long-haul traffic over the Gotthard became heavier and faster, peace suddenly returned to the dusty serpentine route between Göschenen and Airolo. Deep under the mountain, the next chapter in the history of the Gotthard was being written: in early 1882, the first mail trains rolled through the new tunnel, and in May that year, grand opening celebrations were held in Lucerne and Milan. 'The barrier which divided nations has fallen,' announced the Swiss President Simeon Bavier. 'Countries have moved closer to each other, and are now open to world traffic.' Alfred Escher, the disgraced railway pioneer and conqueror

of the great Saint Gotthard, did not attend the inauguration for health reasons. On 1 June 1882, the Gotthard Railway finally started its scheduled operations between Immensee and Chiasso. As early as 1883, more than a million passengers travelled by train through the Gotthard – about as many as those who had crossed the pass during the entire 50 years of the stagecoach era. The volume of goods came to almost half a million tonnes. With the Gotthard Railway, Switzerland had finally become the bridge of Europe; the disadvantage of the internal situation had become, as the historian Ernst Gagliardi wrote in 1939, a transit advantage. 'Without the railway, Switzerland would have long remained an agrarian state out of reach of modern development,' wrote the journalist Helmut Stalder in his 2003-published book Mythos Gotthard. 'The Gotthard Railway turned a dead end into a European hub and gave Switzerland a locational advantage that still determines the structure of the economy today.'

Thanks to the Gotthard Railway, the travel time between Basel and Milan had been shortened from more than two days to just ten hours. However, the railway line not only brought astounding acceleration and opened the door to places beyond the Alps, it also became a destination in itself – as an impressive symbol of man's progress and victory over nature. Every child soon learned of the church tower of Wassen, which travellers passed three times as the steam train chuffed its way up through the spiral tunnels.

And the buffet in the Göschenen railway station, where guests could enjoy a six-course menu during a 25-minute stopover, should have earned itself a place in the country's history books as the first fast food restaurant in Switzerland. In 1909, the Gotthard Railway Company was taken over by SBB, and in the autumn of 1920, the line was finally fully electrified. Many famous Swiss locomotives – such as the particularly powerful mountain-climbing 'Crocodile' – became legendary on the Gotthard route.

With the new railway line, the Gotthard gained immense geo-strategic importance. At the same time, the tense political situation in Europe put increasing pressure on Switzerland. After Austria, Hungary and Germany united in the Triple Alliance in 1882, and, due to the conflict with France, the military march of Italian troops through Switzerland to the north could no longer be excluded. Planning for a central fortification on the Gotthard began under the military Chief of Staff, Alphons Pfyffer von Altishofen, which was built and expanded until 1895. At the same time, the mountain troops in the region were reinforced. Even though the situation did not end up as a defence case, from this point on, the Gotthard stood at the centre of military strategies. Even the narrative of an autonomous, neutral Swiss state, which for centuries had contributed to European peacekeeping through the protection of the Gotthard route, consolidated during this time.

Die Automobilisten kommen

Nach der Eröffnung der Gotthardbahn war der Passverkehr auf der alten Poststraße am Gotthard fast zum Erliegen gekommen. Doch um die Jahrhundertwende wurden die Kurven und Kehren plötzlich von einer ganz neuen Art Reisender heimgesucht – den Automobilisten. 1901 wurde die erste Autofahrt über den Gotthard dokumentiert, und schon kurz darauf im ganzen Urnerland ein Automobilverbot gegen die neuen Herrenfahrer und ihre lärmenden Maschinen erlassen. Nichts von dem Gesetz ahnte 1902 der deutsche Dichter und Car Guy Otto Julius Bierbaum, der den Gotthard in einem einzylindrigen, acht PS starken »Adlerwagen« in nur neun Stunden ohne nennenswerte Pausen überquert hatte und anschließend über die Dorfpolizisten polemisierte, die ihn im Tal für sein Vergehen »verbüsst« hatten: »Zum Glück verstanden wir den Sinn ihrer wütenden Expektorationen nicht, da sie urnerdeutsch fluchten, also in einem Dialekt, der dem ans Hochdeutsche gewöhnten Ohre mehr wie eine unbegreifliche Anhäufung von Rachenlauten denn als eine Abart deutscher Sprache erscheint.« Irgendwann fiel bei Bierbaum jedoch der Groschen: Korrekterweise hätte er in Andermatt einen Ochsen mieten und vor seinen Wagen spannen sollen. Zähneknirschend bezahlte er die fälligen »Zwanzig Fränkli«.

Doch die Urner Behörden dürften der Auseinandersetzungen mit uneinsichtigen Automobilisten und der ausländischen Schlagzeilen, in denen sie als »Strauchdiebe« und »Wegelagerer« beschimpft wurden, schnell überdrüssig geworden sein: 1906 wurde das Automobilverbot schon wieder gelockert. Am Gotthard zählte man in diesem Jahr bereits 270 »Benzinkutschen«, die im Schatten gewaltiger Staubfahnen über die holprigen Naturstraßen preschten und Mensch wie Tier in Angst und Schrecken versetzten. Die Anwohner der Passstraße hielten ihren Widerstand gegen das »stinkende Benzingefährt« nach Kräften aufrecht. Für eine demokratische Wende im automobilen Passverkehr sorgte schließlich die Schweizer Bundespost, die nach dem Ersten Weltkrieg mit dem »Car alpin« auf die alte Poststraße am Gotthard zurückkehrte. Trotz beinharter Federung erfreuten sich die gelben Postautos wachsender Beliebtheit. Doch das Brummen des Car alpin wurde schon bald von ganz anderem Motorendonner übertönt: Ab 1925 verkehrte mit der Ad Astra Aero die erste Fluglinie zwischen Dübendorf bei Zürich nach Mailand. In den metallenen Junkers-Propellermaschine fanden 13 Passagiere Platz, am Steuer saß bei den ersten Flügen noch Walter Mittelholz – schweizer Flugpionier und späterer Direktor der Swissair.

Derweil nahm der Automobilverkehr in der gesamten Schweiz immer weiter zu: 1928 waren im Land bereits mehr als 63.000 Kraftwagen zugelassen, zudem zählte man über 100.000 ausländische Automobile. Am neu eröffneten Klausenpass starteten berühmte Rennfahrer wie Stuck, Fangio und Caracciola zum »Großen Bergpreis

Motorists Arrive

After the opening of the Gotthard Railway, traffic over the pass via the old post road virtually vanished. However, at the turn of the century, the twists and turns suddenly became popular to a completely new kind of traveller – the motorist. In 1901, the first vehicle to traverse the Gotthard was documented, and shortly afterwards an automobile ban was issued throughout the entire Uri district against the new gentlemen drivers and their noisy machines. Unaware of this law, the German poet and car enthusiast, Otto Julius Bierbaum, conquered the Gotthard at the wheel of a single-cylinder, eight-horsepower Adler Phaeton, taking nine hours virtually nonstop to drive from Bellinzona to Brunnen. He was, however, reprimanded by the local police in the valley for his offense and handed a fine. 'Luckily I didn't understand the reason for their furious tirade, because they cursed in Urner German, a dialect that sounded more like an incomprehensible accumulation of throat noises than what the High German ear is accustomed to hearing.' At some point, though, the penny dropped with Bierbaum realising he should have leased an ox in Andermatt and hitched it to his car. Reluctantly, he paid the fine of 20 francs.

Eventually, the Uri authorities very likely grew tired of the clashes with obstinate motorists and the foreign headlines which painted them as 'rogues' and 'highwaymen' and, in 1906, the vehicle ban was lifted. That year 270 'petrol coaches' were counted on the Gotthard, roaring over the bumpy unpaved tracks with a plume of dust trailing behind them, terrifying both man and beast along the way. The inhabitants along the pass road vehemently maintained their resistance to the 'stinking petrol vehicles'.

The Swiss Federal Post Office eventually returned to the old Gotthard postal track with the car alpin after World War I, heralding a democratic turning point for automobile traffic over the pass. Despite its bone-shaking suspension, the yellow postal delivery vehicles enjoyed increasing popularity. However, the chug of the car alpin was soon drowned out by a completely different engine noise: from 1925, Ad Astra Aero became the first airline to operate flights between Dübendorf near Zurich and Milan. Inside the Junkers propeller plane made of sheet-metal, there was room for 13 passengers, and in the cockpit for the maiden flight sat Walter Mittelholz, the Swiss aviation pioneer and eventual director of Swissair.

Meanwhile, automobile traffic continued to increase throughout Switzerland: by 1928 more than 63,000 vehicles had been registered in the country, and more than 100,000 motorcars from abroad were counted. At the newly-opened Klausen Pass, famous racing drivers such as Stuck, Fangio and Caracciola contested the European Hill Climb Grand Prix. Although races were not held on

von Europa«. Auch wenn auf der abenteuerlichen Gotthardpiste kein Rennen ausgetragen wurde, wollten doch immer mehr Fahrer ihren Wagemut und die Zuverlässigkeit ihrer Automobile zwischen Teufelsbrücke und Tremola unter Beweis stellen. Die einst für Pferdekuschen angelegten Fahrstraßen am Gotthard hielten der neuen Belastung nicht lange stand. Ab 1935 wurde die schwer geschundene Passstraße ausgebaut, staubfrei gemacht und etwa in der Tremola mit Granitsteinen gepflastert. Auch zahlreiche Streckungen und Verbreiterungen der Straße an gefährlichen Stellen sowie Neuanlagen von Tunnels und Brücken wurden durchgeführt. Bei Biasca entstand die erste Brücke Europas in Beton-Stahl-Konstruktion. Auch die ersten Fahrbahnbeläge aus Beton wurden in dieser Zeit am Gotthard verlegt. Sämtliche Modernisierungen waren mehr als notwendig: Im Sommer 1936 wurden in Hospental täglich rund 650 Fahrzeuge gezählt, zwei Jahre später waren es – trotz der angespannten politischen Lage in Europa – bereits rund 850 Automobile, Busse, Lastwagen und Motorräder, die jeden Tag über den Pass rollten.

Die »Wacht am Gotthard«

Mit dem Überfall Hitler-Deutschlands auf Polen im Jahr 1939 und dem Ausbruch des Zweiten Weltkrieges kam der Reiseverkehr am Gotthard praktisch zum Erliegen. Nachdem die Nationalsozialisten 1940 in Frankreich einmarschiert waren, rückte der Gotthard schließlich in ganz anderem Kontext ins Zentrum der politischen Aufmerksamkeit: Von faschistischen Ländern eingeschlossen, musste die Schweizer Armeeführung eine Strategie entwickeln, sich auf den drohenden Einmarsch feindlicher Truppen vorzubereiten. Da die Schweizer Armee der deutschen Kriegsmaschinerie im Flachland hoffnungslos unterlegen gewesen wäre, wurde ein neuer Verteidigungsdispositiv entwickelt. Im Juli 1940 informierte General Henri Guisan seine Offiziere beim »Rütlirapport« vor historischer Kulisse über die neue Strategie. Das Konzept des »Réduit national« sah es vor, das Mittelland mit seinen Großstädten und seiner Industrie im Falle eines Angriffes mehr oder weniger kampflos preiszugeben und alle Kräfte auf die Verteidigung des zentralen Alpenraumes, vor allem des Gotthards, und die Zerstörung aller für Deutschland und Italien strategisch wichtigen Nord-Süd-Verbindungen zu konzentrieren. Am Gotthard entstanden daraufhin gewaltige Bunker- und Verteidigungsanlagen, und bereits 1941 hatte fast die gesamte Schweizer Armee in den Alpenfestungen Stellung bezogen.

Ob es die Aussicht eines langen und verlustreichen Kampfes im Hochgebirge war, die Hitler und seine Armee von einem Überfall auf die Schweiz abhielt, oder vielmehr kriegswirtschaftliche Interessen den Ausschlag gaben, wird bis heute von Historikern diskutiert. Die »geistige Landesverteidigung«, die sich im Rückgriff auf die Entstehungsgeschichte der Eidgenossenschaft

the adventurous Gotthard route, more and more drivers were eager to demonstrate their feats of derring-do and the reliability of their vehicles on the stretch between the Devil's Bridge and Tremola. The track that had once been carved out for horse-drawn coaches did not withstand the new stresses for long. From 1935, the badly damaged pass road at the Gotthard was improved, made dust-free and, like in the Tremola, paved with granite stones. Numerous extensions and widening of the road at dangerous points, as well as the installation of new tunnels and bridges, were carried out. Near Biasca, Europe's first bridge of concrete and steel was constructed. The first concrete road surfaces were also laid at this time on the Gotthard. All of these modifications were more than necessary: in the summer of 1936, 650 vehicles were counted in Hospental every day; two years later – despite the tense political situation in Europe – around 850 automobiles, buses, trucks and motorbikes rolled over the pass every day.

The Watch on the Gotthard

With the attack of Poland by Hitler's Germany in 1939 and the outbreak of World War II, traffic on the Gotthard almost came to a standstill. After the Nazis invaded France in 1940, the Gotthard finally moved into the centre of attention politically, albeit in a very different context: hemmed in by fascist countries, the leaders of the Swiss army had to develop strategies to prepare for the threat of invasion by enemy troops. Since the Swiss army would have been hopelessly inferior to the German war machine in the lowlands, a new defence system was developed. In July 1940, General Henri Guisan called his officers to the Rütli to brief them on the new strategy in a historical setting. The concept of the 'Réduit National' (National Redoubt) outlined that, in the event of invasion, the central plateaus and their cities and industries would more or less concede without resistance and instead all defence energies would be focussed on the central Alpine region, especially the Gotthard. All north-south connections that were strategically important to Germany and Italy would be destroyed. Enormous bunker and defence facilities were built on the Gotthard, and by 1941, virtually the entire Swiss army had taken up position in the Alpine fortresses.

Still today, historians are discussing whether it was the prospect of a long and costly battle in the mountains or the economic interests of war that was the decisive factor in preventing Hitler and his army from invading Switzerland. In any case, the 'spirit of the country's defence', with its roots in the founding of the Swiss Confederation around the Gotthard, traceable to the century-old tradition of the struggle for freedom, was continued during the Cold War. Only after the fall of the Iron Curtain were the bunkers on the Gotthard abandoned by the Swiss military in the late 1990s.

am Gotthard auf eine Jahrhunderte alte Tradition des Freiheitskampfes berief, wurde jedoch auch im Kalten Krieg fortgesetzt. Erst nach dem Fall des Eisernen Vorhangs wurden die Bunkeranlagen am Gotthard in den späten 1990er-Jahren vom Schweizerischen Militär aufgegeben.

Der Verkehrsteufel kehrt zurück

Nach Ende der Zweiten Weltkrieges lag Europa in Trümmern – doch mit dem Wiederaufbau kehrte auch der Reiseverkehr zurück. Schon Ende der 1940er-Jahre hatte die Zahl ausländischer Fahrzeuge in der Schweiz die Höchstwerte der Vorkriegszeit überschritten. Im Sommer 1948 wurden täglich bereits mehr als 500 Automobile und Motorräder am Gotthardpass gezählt, 1955 waren es mehr als 2.800 Fahrzeuge pro Tag. Ein Jahrzehnt später schob und staute sich zwischen Mai und Oktober bereits eine Blechlawine von mehr als 880.000 Fahrzeugen über die Passhöhe. Die Zeit des Massentourismus hatte begonnen – und der Gotthard war das Nadelöhr auf dem Weg an die Seen und Strände Italiens. In Uri wurde derweil gespottet, der Teufel habe späte Rache geübt für den Verrat beim Bau der Schöllenenbrücke und hülle das Tal nun in eine höllische Wolke aus Abgasen und Benzingestank. Bereits 1950 malte der Urner Künstler Heinrich Danioth in der Schöllenen einen roten Satan samt Ziegenbock an die Felswand. Doch der Fortschrittsteufel ließ sich nicht mehr bannen.

Schon in den 1940er-Jahren war die Ausbesserung der alten Poststraße fortgesetzt und zwischen 1949 und 1952 die alte Tremola mit Granitsteinen und Beton endgültig ausgebaut worden. Doch den Kantonen war bald klar, dass die Straße dem rasant anwachsenden Verkehrsaufkommen nicht lange standhalten würde. Zwischen 1951 und 1956 wurde die Schöllenenschlucht mit einer modernen Fahrstraße samt Tunnel erschlossen und eine größere Teufelsbrücke über die Reuss gebaut. Auch die neue, 7,5 Meter breite Straße hinauf nach Hospental und zur Kantonsgrenze verließ mit neuen Tunnels und Kehren die Spuren des alten Säumerweges; Andermatt wurde ab 1969 umfahren. Auf Tessiner Seite entstanden in den 1950er- und 1960er-Jahren zahlreiche neue Streckenabschnitte wie die Mont-Ceneri-Straße, die Umfahrung der alten Passgebäude und das eindrucksvolle, 8,5 Kilometer lange Straßenstück, das von der Passhöhe über 13 Brücken und Viadukte, durch zwei Tunnels und eine Lawinengalerie elegant ins Bedrettotal hineinschwingt und schließlich kurz vor Motto Bartola endet. In den 1970er-Jahren wurde schließlich mithilfe großer Brücken und Viadukte die Verbindung nach Airolo neu angelegt.

Der längste Straßentunnel der Welt

Mit der Eröffnung der neuen Straßenstücke hatte der Passverkehr 1971 mit mehr als 950.000 Fahrzeugen seinen Höchststand erreicht. Wer der Automobilkarawane

Traffic Chaos Returns

After the end of the Second World War, Europe was in tatters – but with its reconstruction, tourist traffic returned. By the end of the 1940s, the number of foreign vehicles visiting Switzerland had exceeded the highest pre-war figures. In summer 1948, more than 500 cars and motorbikes crossed the Gotthard every day. In 1955, it was more than 2,800 vehicles per day. A decade later, more than 880,000 vehicles jammed their way over the Gotthard Pass between May and October in a snaking line of sheet-metal. The era of mass tourism had arrived – and the Gotthard was the bottleneck on the way to the lakes and beaches of Italy. Meanwhile, in Uri, it was said that this was the devil's late revenge for the betrayal in the building of the Schöllenen Bridge and that now the valley was blanketed in a hellish cloud of exhaust fumes. In 1950, the Uri artist Heinrich Danioth painted a red devil with a goat on a rock wall in the Schöllenen. This time, however, the demon of progress could not be stopped.

In the 1940s, repairs to the old post road had been continued, and between 1949 and 1952, the old Tremola with its granite pavers and concrete was finally updated. But the cantons soon realised that the road would not hold up against the rapidly increasing traffic. Between 1951 and 1956, the Schöllenen Gorge was opened with a modern road surface including a tunnel and a wider Devil's Bridge built over the Reuss. The new, 7.5-metre-wide road up to Hospental to the canton border veered from the old bridle path with new tunnels and hairpins, and from 1969, Andermatt was bypassed. On the Ticino side, many new sections were created in the 1950s and 1960s, such as the Monte Ceneri Road, which bypassed the old pass buildings and the impressive 8.5-kilometre stretch of road that meandered elegantly from the pass summit over 13 bridges and viaducts, through two tunnels and an avalanche protection gallery into the Bedretto Valley and ended just before Motto Bartola. In the 1970s, the connection to Airolo was finally rebuilt featuring large bridges and viaducts.

The World's Longest Road Tunnel

With the opening of new passages, the pass traffic had reached its peak in 1971 with more than 950,000 vehicles. Those who wanted to avoid the caravan of cars at the pass could take the car shuttle train through the tunnel – but in the high season had to queue for hours in the loading yards. In any case, the Gotthard Pass Road, as the most important Alpine transit link, was already in decline. In 1960, autobahn construction had gathered momentum in Switzerland. With the national N2 road between Basel, Lucerne, the Gotthard, Lugano and Chiasso, a brand-new, winter-proof, north-south transport route was to be built. As early as the 1930s, the architect Paul Hosch had played with the idea of a road tunnel through the Gotthard massif – now the plans were to become re-

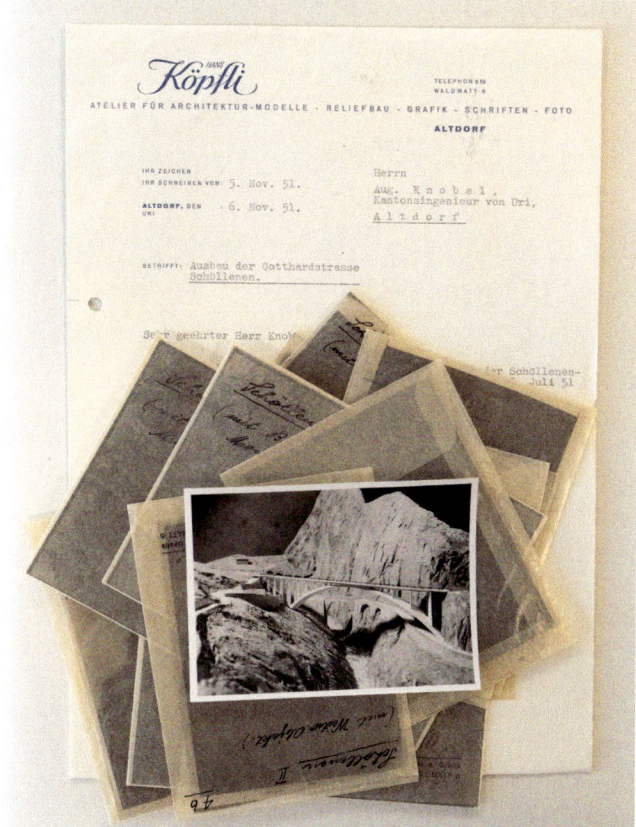

MIT FREUNDLICHER GENEHMIGUNG
COURTESY OF:
KANTON URI STAATSARCHIV

am Pass entgehen wollte, konnte sich per Autozug durch den Tunnel transportieren lassen – musste dafür in den Hochsaison aber stundenlang an den Verladebahnhöfen warten. Die Gotthardpassstraße als wichtigster Alpenübergang war ohnehin bereits im Niedergang. Schon 1960 hatte in der Schweiz der Autobahnbau an Fahrt aufgenommen. Mit der Nationalstraße N2 sollte zwischen Basel, Luzern, dem Gotthard, Lugano und Chiasso eine völlig neue, wintersichere Transitautobahn für den Nord-Süd-Verkehr entstehen. Schon in den 1930er-Jahren hatte der Architekt Paul Hosch mit der Idee eines Straßentunnels durch das Gotthardmassiv gespielt – nun wurde die Planung erneut konkret. 1965 war der Tunnelbau beschlossene Sache, 1968 entschied sich das Schweizer Parlament gegen einen kürzeren Scheiteltunnel und für einen 16,9 Kilometer langen, einröhrigen Straßentunnel mit Sicherheitsstollen zwischen Göschenen und Airolo. 1970 begannen die Bauarbeiten. 1973 musste der Teufelsstein verschoben werden, er lag auf der Trasse der projektierten Autobahn. 1980 war der Gotthardtunnel vollendet – als längster Straßentunnel der Welt. Einmal mehr hatte der Straßenbau am Gotthard einen Superlativ geschaffen.

In seiner Eröffnungsrede ließ es sich Bundesrat Hans Hürlimann nicht nehmen, die Bedeutung des Tunnelbaus als weiteres Schlüsselbauwerk in der Geschichte des Gotthards herauszustellen: Nach der Öffnung der Schöllenen um 1200, die zur Gründung der Eidgenossenschaft geführt hatte, und dem Bau der Poststraße sowie der Gotthardbahn im 19. Jahrhundert, die der Schweiz ein neues verkehrspolitisches Gewicht verliehen hatten, sei mit der neuen Autobahn durch den Berg »ein neues, kräftiges Glied geschmiedet für die unerlässliche Verbindung unseres an Kulturgütern reichen Südens an das Verkehrsnetz und die Wirtschaft des Nordens.« Erneut war der Gotthard zudem zum Schauplatz einer außerordentlichen Beschleunigung geworden: Hatte man den Pass im eigenen Auto bisher nur mühsam und mit viel Geduld überwinden können, durchfuhr man das zentrale Alpenmassiv nun ganz bequem und ließ das »erschröckliche Gebirge«, das Reisende viele Jahrhunderte lang mit Furcht erfüllt hatte, nach 15 Minuten Fahrt durch die Tunnelröhre hinter sich. Allerdings hatte der Fortschritt auch seinen Preis: Das erhebende Gefühl, am Gotthardpass nach beschwerlicher Fahrt die Pforte zwischen Ländern und Kulturen, zwischen Nord und Süd zu durchschreiten, verblasste im Neonschein des Tunnels zu einer alltäglichen Banalität. »Man kann die Alpen seit einiger Zeit immer schneller überfliegen oder sie in Straßentunnels unterfahren«, schrieb Richard Zürcher schon 1971 in seinem Schweizer Reiseführer. »Trotzdem locken die Pässe, und auch ihre Zufahrten bilden ein besonderes Erlebnis. Es ist das Glück der Annäherung, das sich bei langsamem Durchqueren der Alpen offenbart, ein Glück des langsamen, jeden Abschnitt auskostenden Reisenden, das doch immer durch die Vorfreude auf das Ziel hin bestimmt ist.«

ality. In 1965, construction of the tunnel was a done deal. In 1968, the Swiss parliament decided against a shorter summit tunnel and instead opted for a 16.9-kilometre-long tunnel consisting of one bidirectional tube with escape route side tunnels. Construction work began in 1970. In 1973, the Devil's Rock had to be moved as it lay in the path of the projected autobahn. In 1980, the Gotthard Tunnel was finished – it was the longest road tunnel in the world. Once again, road building on the Gotthard had set the benchmark.

In the inauguration speech, Federal Councillor Hans Hürlimann grabbed the chance to emphasise the importance of the tunnel construction as another key undertaking at the Gotthard. After the opening of the Schöllenen around the year 1200, which led to the founding of the Confederation, as well as the construction of the Post Road and the Gotthard Railway in the 19th century, which had lent new weight to Switzerland's transport policy, the latest highway through the mountain was a 'new, powerful link for the indispensable connection of the culturally rich heritage in the south to the transport network and economy of the north.'

Once again, the Gotthard had become the scene of extraordinary acceleration: while crossing the pass in one's own car had previously required immense effort and patience, now one could travel through the central massif in relative comfort and leave the 'terrifying mountains' – that had filled travellers with trepidation for many centuries – behind after a 15-minute drive through the tunnel. Progress, however, came at a price: the uplifting feeling of having conquered the arduous Gotthard passage through the doorway between countries and cultures, between the north and south, faded into everyday banality in the harsh neon lights of the tunnel. 'For some time now, you can fly over the Alps at an ever increasing pace or drive under them in road tunnels,' wrote Richard Zürcher in his Swiss travel guide of 1971. 'Nevertheless, the passes are alluring, and the roads there are always a special experience. It is the joy of approaching that is revealed in the slow crossing of the Alps, the joy of the slow traveller who lingers over every stretch, yet always pushes on in anticipation of the destination.'

The Limits of Growth

Moreover, with traffic increasing, the Gotthard Road Tunnel did not always allow a free run, but soon turned into another bottleneck. While in 1981 almost three million vehicles took the tunnel route, by 1990 the number was up to a good 5.5 million vehicles and peaked in 2000 to around 6.8 million vehicles. In 2016, more than half of all vehicles crossed the Swiss Alps through the Gotthard – around 17,000 automobiles and trucks per day. And although an interval feed system has regulated the transit traffic since the 2001 tunnel fire, it is mainly trucks more than anything that are pushing the one-lane Gotthard

Die Grenzen des Wachstums

Hinzu kam, dass der Gotthard-Straßentunnel mit zunehmendem Verkehr nicht immer freie Fahrt versprach, sondern bald selbst zum Nadelöhr wurde. Waren 1981 noch knapp 3 Millionen Fahrzeuge pro Jahr durch den Tunnel gefahren, zählte man 1990 bereits gut 5,5 Millionen und im Spitzenjahr 2000 rund 6,8 Millionen Fahrzeuge. 2016 querten mehr als die Hälfte aller Fahrzeuge die schweizerischen Alpen durch den Gotthard – rund 17.000 Automobile und Lastwagen pro Tag. Auch wenn seit dem Tunnelbrand des Jahres 2001 ein Tropfenzählersystem die Frequenzen für den Transitgüterverkehr begrenzt, sind es vor allem die Lastwagen, die den einspurig befahrbaren Gotthardtunnel schnell an die Grenzen seiner Kapazitäten bringen. Erfahrene Gotthardreisende wissen heute: Wer vor dem Tunnel in einen der berüchtigten Staus gerät und nicht früh genug in Richtung San Bernardino oder auf die alte Gotthard-Passstraße abzweigt, kann alle Hoffnung fahren lassen. 2017 zählte man am Südportal des Tunnels 196 Stautage. Im Mai 2018 wurde am gesperrten Gotthard sogar ein »Superstau« mit 28 Kilometern Länge gemessen.

Schon 1994 hatte das Schweizer Stimmvolk die sogenannte »Alpeninitiative« zum Schutze des Alpengebietes vor dem Transitverkehr angenommen. Um den Güterverkehr noch effizienter auf die Schiene verlagern zu können, wurde 1999 mit dem Bau eines 57 Kilometer langen »Basistunnels« zwischen Erstfeld in Uri und Bodio im Tessin begonnen, 2010 erfolgte der Durchstich. 2016 wurde die neue Eisenbahn-Alpentraversale durch das Gotthardmassiv als längster Eisenbahntunnel der Welt in Betrieb genommen. Auch für den Personenverkehr brachte der Basistunnel eine entscheidende Beschleunigung – die Reise mit dem Zug von Zürich nach Mailand hatte sich von 3 Stunden und 40 Minuten um eine ganze Stunde verkürzt. Im Jahr der Eröffnung wurde auch der Bau einer zweiten Straßenröhre durch den Gotthard beschlossen, um den Verkehr während der nötig gewordenen Sanierung des ersten Gotthard-Straßentunnel aus dem Jahr 1980 umzuleiten. Ob die Schweizer Politik ihr Versprechen einhalten kann, die beiden Röhren auch in Zukunft bloß einspurig befahren zu lassen und somit die Kapazitäten am Gotthard für den europäischen Transitverkehr künstlich zu begrenzen, wird sich zeigen. In den gut 800 Jahren seit Öffnung der Schöllenen kannte die Verkehrsentwicklung am Gotthard bis auf kurze Einbrüche eigentlich nur eine Richtung – nach oben. Oder um es frei nach Carl Spitteler zu sagen: Führt ein neuer und größerer Weg in die Speisekammer, werden die Ameisen sich nicht lange bitten lassen.

Vom Transitraum zur Tourismus-Destination

Die alte Gotthard-Passstraße erfreut sich derweil wachsender Beliebtheit: 2015 überqueren fast 1.500 Fahrzeuge pro Tag die Passhöhe. Mit dem Nationalen Gotthard-Mu-

tunnel to its limits. Seasoned Gotthard travellers know that those who get caught up in one of the notorious traffic jams before the tunnel and miss the turnoff to San Bernardino or the old Gotthard Pass Road might as well abandon all hope. In 2017, there were 196 days of traffic jams at the southern end of the tunnel. In May 2018, a 28-kilometre-long 'mega tailback' was measured on the closed Gotthard.

As early as 1994, Swiss voters had adopted the so-called 'Alpine initiative' to protect the Alpine region from transit traffic. In order to be able to transfer the transport of goods even more efficiently to rail, the construction of a 57-kilometre 'base tunnel' between Erstfeld in Uri and Bodio in Ticino began in 1999, with final breakthrough in 2010. In 2016, the new Alpine railway link through the Gotthard massif went into operation as the longest railway tunnel in the world. The base tunnel also allowed a faster passage for passengers – with the train from Zurich to Milan shaving an entire hour off the three hour, 40 minute trip.

During the year of its opening, the decision was made for a second road tunnel through the Gotthard to redirect traffic during the necessary renovations of the first Gotthard road tunnel finished in 1980. Whether Swiss policy can live up to its promise of leaving the two tubes with just one-lane in each direction in the future and thus artificially capping the capacity at the Gotthard for European transit traffic, remains to be seen. In the 800 years since the opening of the Schöllenen to recent times, the traffic trend on the Gotthard has moved in only one direction – upwards. Or to quote Carl Spitteler: If a new and larger trail leads into the pantry, the ants won't take long in coming.

From Transit to Tourism

In the meantime, the old Gotthard Pass Road is becoming increasingly popular: in 2015, almost 1,500 vehicles a day traversed the pass. With the National Gotthard Museum in the 'Alte Sust' and the Ospizio San Gottardo, which was renovated and modernised in 2010 by the Basel-based architectural firm Miller & Maranta, the pass itself is once again becoming an interesting tourist destination. In the Sasso San Gottardo museum in the old artillery fortification near the pass summit, visitors can also take an impressive journey through time into the past bunker life of soldiers. The Tremola Road, too, was renovated in 2011, after frost and avalanches had severely damaged the integrity of the road. Preservationists were critical, however, that the canton of Ticino had not shown sensitivity in the restoration of the historic road – and replaced the old dry stone walls that support the steep corners with concrete cores in various places.

This conflict exemplifies the balancing act between operational requirements of modern transit traffic and

MIT FREUNDLICHER GENEHMIGUNG
COURTESY OF:
KANTON URI STAATSARCHIV

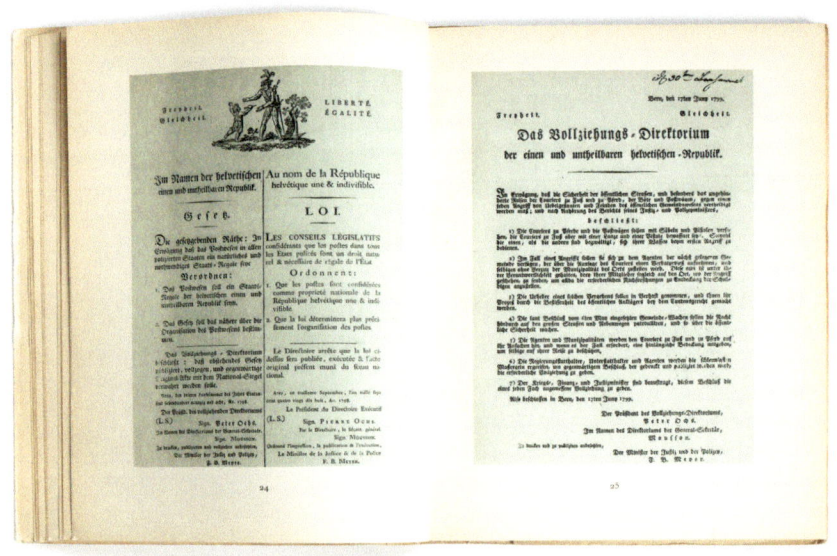

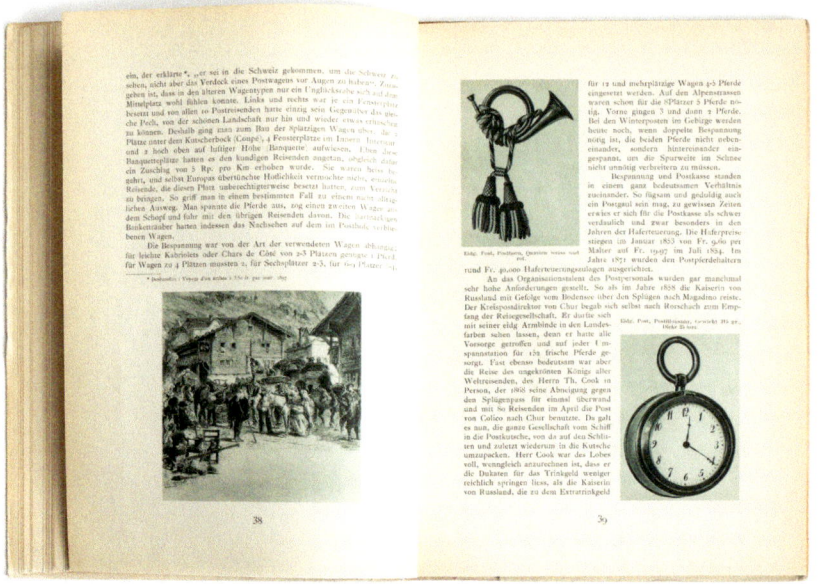

Car alpin der Bauart des Jahres 1919. Offene Karosserie mit teilweise Rückwärtssitzen, Vollgummireifen, 40 PS Motor, Malojapoststrasse (St. Moritz-Castasegna).

Car alpin aus dem Jahre 1923. Spezialbauart für das Befahren enger Kehren, erste Versuche mit Luftreifen. Poststrasse Schuls-Landeck.

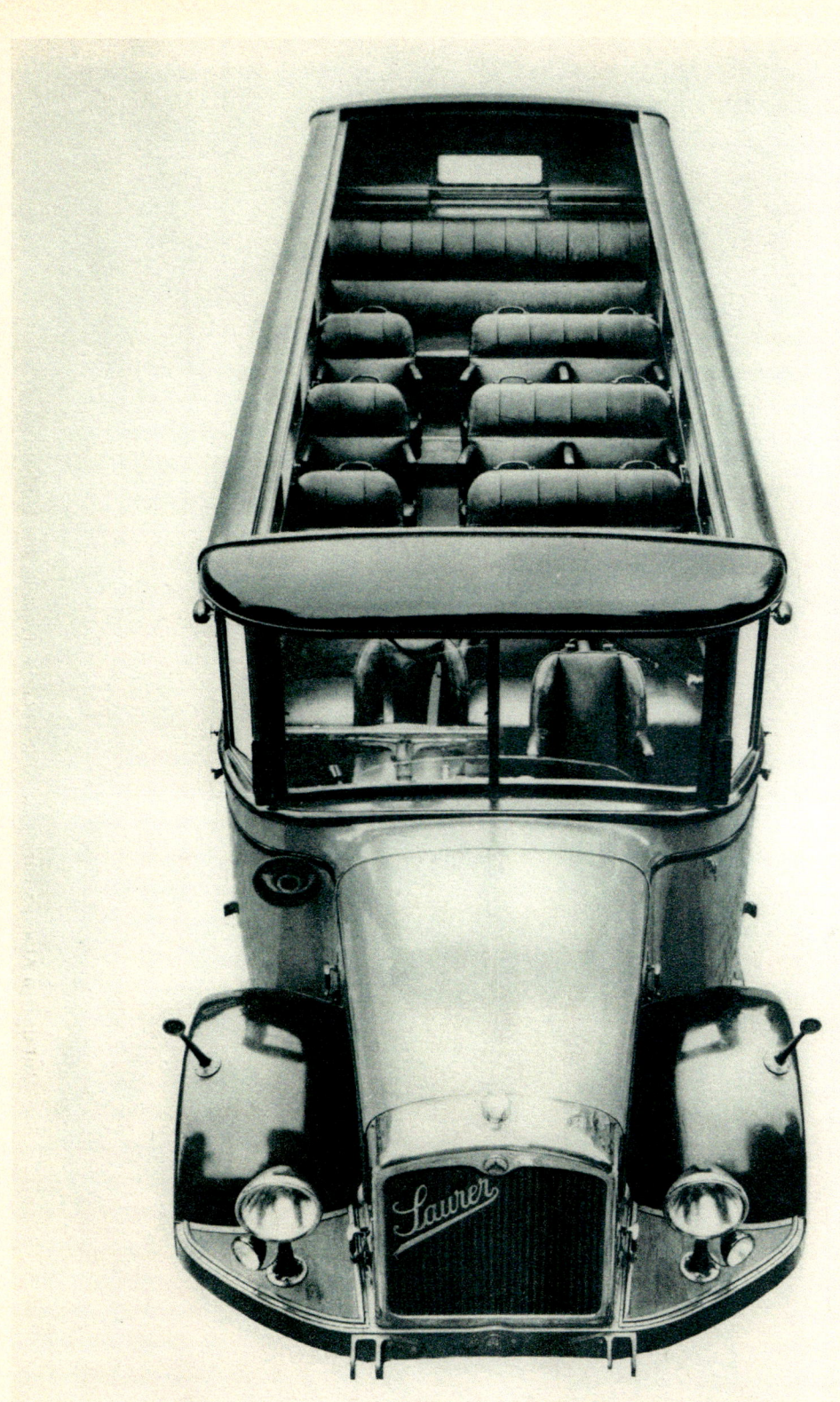

Motor 100 PS. Tiefrahmenfahrgestell. Ausserordentlich wirkungsvolle Bremsanlage. Karosserie mit elektrischem Rollverdeck, Klubfauteuilbestuhlung, moderne Heizungs- und Beleuchtungseinrichtungen.

59

Postauto mit Raupenbandantrieb, Bauart 1930. Allwetterkarosserie mit 7 Plätzen. Poststrasse Chur-Tschiertschen.

69

Schneeschleuder, Rückansicht mit dem Stahlraupenantrieb und dem zweiten Motor für den Antrieb der Schaufelräder.

Schneeschleuder in Tätigkeit, beiderseitiger Schneeauswurf.

seum in der »Alten Sust« und dem 2010 sanierten, durch das Basler Architekturbüro Miller & Maranta modern erweiterten Ospizio San Gottardo ist der Pass selbst wieder zu einem interessanten Reiseziel geworden. Im Museum Sasso San Gottardo in der alten Artilleriefestung nahe der Passhöhe kann man zudem eine eindrückliche Zeitreise in das einstige Bunkerleben der Soldaten unternehmen. Auch die alte Tremolastraße wurde im Jahr 2011 saniert, nachdem Frost und Lawinen die Substanz der Straße stark angegriffen hatten. Denkmalschützer kritisierten jedoch, der Kanton Tessin habe bei der Instandsetzung nicht jenes Fingerspitzengefühl gezeigt, dass im Umgang mit der historischen Straße geboten gewesen sei – und die alten Trockenmauern, welche die Kurven stützen, an verschiedenen Orten durch Betonkerne ersetzt.

Die Auseinandersetzung ist exemplarisch für den Spagat zwischen betrieblichen Erfordernissen des modernen Transitverkehrs und konservatorischen Ansprüchen an ein viele Jahrhunderte altes, äußerst bedeutsames Monument der europäischen Kulturgeschichte, der am Gotthardpass noch größer ist als an den meisten anderen Alpenübergängen. Eine Bewerbung um den Welterbe-Status durch die UNESCO, wie ihn beispielsweise die Großglockner Hochalpenstraße in Österreich anstrebt, wird am Gotthard eher mit Blick auf die historische Bahnstrecke diskutiert. Und doch gibt es immer wieder Bestrebungen, das Gotthardgebiet von einer reinen Durchgangsregion in eine Tourismusdestination zu verwandeln.

Seit 2009 treibt der ägyptisch-montenegrinische Unternehmer Samih Sawiris seine Pläne voran, auf einem alten Militärgelände bei Andermatt einen mondänen Urlaubsort für internationale Gäste entstehen zu lassen. Auch ein Zusammenschluss der Tourismusräume von Brig bis Chur und von Altdorf bis Bellinzona mit seinen zahlreichen Wanderwegen und Skipisten zu einer gemeinschaftlichen Region wird weiter verfolgt. Doch die Gotthardregion hält noch einen weiteren Trumpf in der Hand: Mit Furka, Nufenen, Grimsel, Lukmanier, Oberalp, Susten, Klausen und Gotthard verbinden sich in der Region acht historische Alpenpässe zu einem wahren Vergnügungspark für Kurvenliebhaber. Egal ob mit dem Rennrad, auf dem Sattel des »Töffs« oder am Steuer eines alpentauglichen Sportwagens – in wenigen Tagen kann man rund um den Gotthard die vielleicht schönste Bergrundfahrt der Welt unternehmen. Es bleibt zu hoffen, dass mit wachsendem Bewusstsein für die Geschichte dieser einzigartigen Kulturlandschaft auch der Respekt für die Bergwelt zunimmt – und moderne Passfahrer die Kurven, Kehren und Serpentinen mit jener Umsicht erfahren, die angesichts der historischen Dimension und Verletzlichkeit der alpinen Natur angebracht ist. Wie Generationen von Reisenden zuvor fügen schließlich auch wir einen kleinen Faden zum großen Erzählstoff der Gotthard-Geschichte hinzu.

Eine Bewerbung um den Welterbe-Status durch die UNESCO, wie ihn beispielsweise die Großglockner Hochalpenstraße in Österreich anstrebt, wird am Gotthard eher mit Blick auf die historische Bahnstrecke diskutiert.

An application for World Heritage status by UNESCO, like the Grossglockner High Alpine Road in Austria, is under discussion for the Gotthard, specifically with a view to its historic railway line.

---

conservational demands on the centuries-old, extremely important monument of European cultural history, which is even more difficult at the Gotthard Pass than on most other Alpine crossings. An application for World Heritage status by UNESCO, like the Grossglockner High Alpine Road in Austria, is under discussion for the Gotthard, specifically with a view to its historic railway line. And yet, there are ongoing efforts to transform the Gotthard from purely a thoroughfare route into a tourist destination in itself. Since 2009, the Egyptian-Montenegrin entrepreneur Samih Sawiris has been pushing ahead with plans to create a chic holiday destination for international guests at an old military site near Andermatt. A merger of tourism areas from Brig to Chur and Altdorf to Bellinzona with its wide network of hiking trails and ski slopes into one region is being pursued.

But the Gotthard region holds yet another trump card: with the Furka, Nufenen, Grimsel, Lukmanier, Oberalp, Susten, Klausen and Gotthard, eight historic Alpine passes in the region combine to form a natural amusement park for admirers of snaking roads. Whether on the saddle of a racing bike or motorcycle or at the wheel of an alpine-suitable sports car, within just a few days, travellers can explore arguably the world's most beautiful mountain drives around the Gotthard. One can only hope that with growing awareness of the history of this unique cultural landscape, respect for the mountains will also grow – and modern travellers will experience the curves, bends and serpentines with due admiration befitting of the historical dimension and vulnerability of alpine nature. Like generations of travellers before, we add a tiny thread to the great fabric of the Gotthard story.

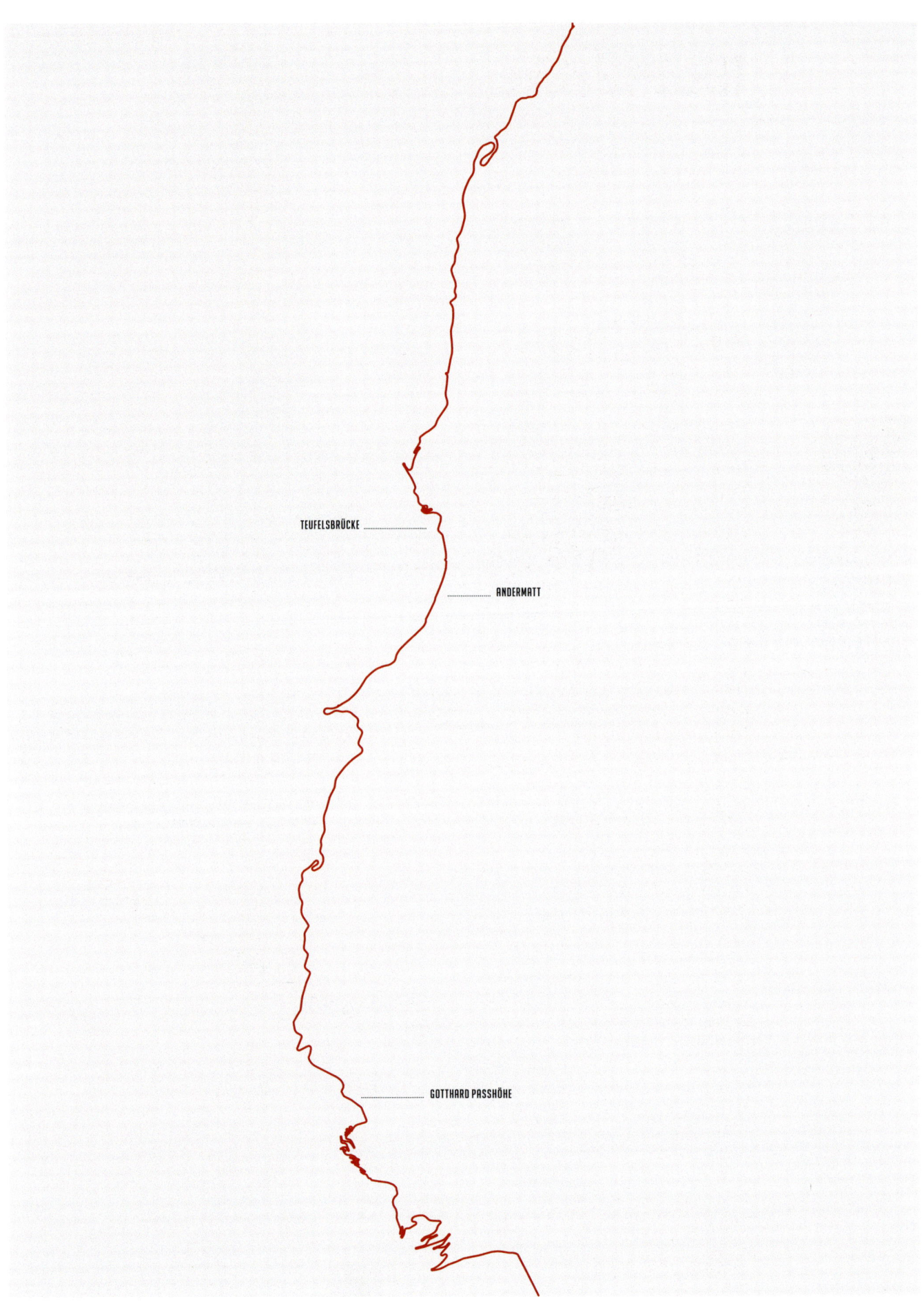

DIE STRECKE

THE ROUTE

Der Gotthardpass ist Teil der rund 110 Kilometer langen Gotthardstrasse, die Altdorf im Kanton Uri mit Airolo im Kanton Tessin verbindet. Das Erlebnis einer Fahrt über den Gotthard von Norden nach Süden beginnt aber eigentlich schon früher – bei der Anreise. Entlang des Vierwaldstättersees über die Axenstraße mit ihren Galerien, Tunnels und atemberaubenden Ausblicken führend, ist sie allerfeinstes Warm-up für den Pass. Am Südufer des Sees angekommen, ist das Reusstal noch weit und hell. Doch folgt man der alten Hauptstrasse 2 weiter nach Erstfeld, Silenen, dem Eingang zum Maderanertal, Gurtnellen und Wassen, verengt sich das Tal zunehmend, bis in Göschenen die Felswände rechts und links der Reussschlucht dramatisch-alpin in den Himmel ragen. Hier, wo der 1973 um 127 Meter nach Norden verschobene Teufelsstein die Autofahrer am Tunnelportal an die Entstehungsgeschichte der Straße erinnert, beginnt auch der markanteste Abschnitt der Passstraße über den Gotthard.

Noch bevor die Straße am Schöllenentor mit ihrer ersten Kehrenkombination an Höhe gewinnt, zeugt rechter Hand die steinerne Händerlisbrücke von der goldenen Epoche des Saumhandels im 17. Jahrhundert, während weiter oben am Berg die Galerien der Gotthardbahn an die Ingenieurskunst der Eisenbahnpioniere der Belle Époque erinnert. Durch dunkle Lawinengalerien geht es weiter hinauf, bis man auf Höhe des Reuss-Wasserfalls am Bäzberg die vier spektakulärsten Kehren der Nordrampe durchfährt. Das brutalistische Betongetüm weit oben am Fels ist übrigens kein Teil einer alten Wehranlage, sondern ein Lüftungsschacht des Autobahntunnels, der in der Tiefe verläuft. Der Bäzberg

The Gotthard Pass is a section of the 110-kilometre-long Gotthard Road that links Altdorf in the canton of Uri with Airolo in the canton of Ticino. However, the experience of the journey over the Gotthard from north to south actually begins much earlier. The trip along the Axenstrasse at Lake Lucerne with its rock-fall galleries, tunnels and stunning vistas makes for a wonderful warm-up for the pass. At the southern shore of the lake, the Reuss Valley is still wide and verdant. However, following the old Hauptstrasse 2 through Erstfeld, Silenen, the entrance to Maderanertal, Gurtnellen and Wassen, the valley gradually narrows until in Göschenen the rock walls to the right and left of the Reuss Gorge tower almost vertically into the sky. It is here, where the Devil's Rock, which was shifted 127 metres to the north in 1973, reminds motorists at the tunnel entrance, where the most distinctive section of the pass road over the Gotthard begins, of the founding history of the road.

Even before the road at the Schöllenen gateway starts to ascend with the first stack of sweeping curves, the stone Händerlisbrücke on the right bears testimony to the golden age of the bridle paths in the 17th century, while further up the mountain, the Gotthard Railway galleries are reminiscent of the railway pioneers' engineering feats of the Belle Époque. The route continues through dark avalanche galleries to four of the most spectacular switchbacks on the northern approach at the height of the Reuss waterfall at the Bäzberg. The formidable concrete structure high up on the rock is not part of an old weir system, but rather a ventilation shaft for the motorway tunnel

mit seinen steilen Felsstürzen zur Schöllenenschlucht galt bis ins frühe 13. Jahrhundert als unüberwindliches Hindernis – seit den 1950er-Jahren durchfährt man ihn durch einen kurzen Tunnel und überquert dann auf der modernen Teufelsbrücke gefahrlos die tosenden Wasser der Reuss. Nur der rote, vom Künstler Heinrich Danioth an die Felswand gemalte Teufel erinnert den Transitverkehr an die diabolische Legende um die Entstehung des »stiebenden Steges«. Es lohnt sich, hier kurz Halt zu machen, über die alte Steinbrücke aus dem Jahr 1830 zu spazieren und durch einen alten Militärtunnel bis zum Aussichtsplattform Bäzberg heraufzuklettern, wo einem trotz der Höhe die Gischt der Reuss das Gesicht benetzt und sich ein herrlicher Ausblick auf beide Teufelsbrücken sowie die Trasse der Gotthardbahn bietet. In der Kurve oberhalb der alten Teufelsbrücke erinnert zudem das Suworow-Denkmal an den russischen General und die erbitterten Kämpfe russisch-österreichischer Koalitionstruppen und naopleonischer Soldaten im Jahr 1799.

Setzt man seine Fahrt fort, durchquert man den Chilchberg – an dessen nassen Fels gelehnt einst die berüchtigte Twärrenbrücke über den Wildwassern der Reuss schwebte – durch einen weiteren, unscheinbaren Tunnel. Dass dieses »Urner Loch« schon 1708 als erster Tunnelbau der Alpen in den Berg gesprengt wurde und mit ihm die Erfolgsgeschichte des Gotthards erst wirklich Fahrt aufnahm, wissen wohl nur die wenigsten Reisenden. Nach einer weiteren Lawinengalerie erreicht man bei Andermatt schließlich das Urserental – und staunt über die mit einem Mal völlig veränderte Landschaft: Ragten vor wenigen Augenblicken noch schroffe Felswände in den Himmel, ist das Hochtal nun weit und licht, mit sattgrünen Matten auf sanft ansteigenden Hängen. Erst nach dem Dörfchen Hospental wird die Topografie wieder alpiner. Nach einigen engen Kehren windet sich die Straße nun an einem Steilhang entlang des wilden Flussbetts der Gotthardreuss durch das felsig-alpine Hochland in Richtung Passhöhe. Beim Restaurant Gotthard-Mätteli gewinnt die Straße durch eine Doppelkehre nochmals an Höhe, dann erreicht man bereits die Kantonsgrenze zwischen Uri und Tessin. Kurz darauf zweigt die »Strada Vecchia«, die alte Gotthardstraße, ab. Von der modernen Schnellstraße aus lässt sich der Verlauf der alten Poststraße mit ihrem Naturstein-Mauerwerk und ihren einfachen Begrenzungssteinen durch die von Felsen, Schneefeldern, braunen Wiesen und kleinen Seen geprägten Passlandschaft bestens verfolgen.

Schließlich vereinigt sich die »Strada Vecchia« wieder mit der modernen Schnellstraße, und man erblickt linkerhand den Lago di Piazza und dahinter die Gebäude an der Passhöhe auf 2.108 Metern über dem Meer. In der »Alten Sust«, wo zu Zeiten des Saumhandels die Waren eingelagert und die Saumtiere gewechselt wurden, findet sich heute ein Museum zur Geschichte der Passstraße. Neues Zentrum des Gebäudeensembles ist jedoch das

running deep below the Earth's surface. The Bäzberg, with its steep walls and rock falls into the Schöllenen Gorge, was considered an insurmountable obstacle until the early 13th century, however, since the 1950s, it can be crossed via a short tunnel and then over the raging river on the modern-day Devil's Bridge. Only the red devil, painted on the rock wall by the artist Heinrich Danioth, reminds travellers of the diabolical legend underlying the creation of the Stiebende Steg.

It pays to take a short break here and wander over the old stone bridge from 1830, through the former military tunnel and up to the Bäzberg viewing platform. Despite the altitude, the spray from the wild Reuss can be felt on the face and the view of the Devil's Bridge and the lines of the Gotthard Railway are spectacular. In the curve above the old Devil's Bridge, the Suvorov monument commemorates the Russian General and the fierce battles of the Russian-Austrian coalition forces and the Napoleonic army in 1799.

Continuing on, the route crosses the Chilchberg – where the notorious Twärrenbrücke once leaned on the wet rocks over the wild whitewater of the Reuss – and leads through another inconspicuous tunnel. Only very few travellers realise that the "Urner Loch" was the first tunnel construction to be blown into the Alps in 1708 and thus wrote the first chapter in the success story of the Gotthard. After another avalanche gallery, one finally reaches the Ursern Valley near Andermatt. The sudden change in the landscape is astounding here: while a few moments earlier dark, jagged cliffs towered into the sky, here the high mountain valley now opens up, flooded with light, with the gentle slopes carpeted in lush green meadows. Only after the small hamlet of Hospental does the topography become alpine again. After several tight hairpins, the road weaves its way along the steep cliff of the wild Gotthard Reuss river bed through the rocky alpine plateau towards the top of the pass. At the Gotthard-Mätteli Restaurant the road gains more altitude through a double switchback, before arriving at the canton border between Uri and Ticino. Shortly afterwards, the Strada Vecchia – the old Gotthard Road – branches off. Viewed from the modern highway, travellers can savour the old Post Road with its natural stone walls and simple boundary stones through the pass landscape dominated by rocks, snowfields, tundra grasslands and small lakes.

Finally, the Strada Vecchia rejoins the highway. To the left lies the Lago della Piazza, with the pass buildings at 2,108 metres above sea level on the far shore. In the Alte Sust, where goods were once stored during the mule-train days and pack animals were exchanged, one discovers a museum highlighting the history of the pass road. At the heart of the group of buildings is the hospice, which has been masterfully renovated by Miller & Maranta and seems to merge with the landscape like a

Es lohnt sich, hier kurz Halt zu machen, über die alte Steinbrücke aus dem Jahr 1830 zu spazieren und durch einen alten Militärtunnel bis zum Aussichtsplattform Bäzberg heraufzuklettern, wo einem trotz der Höhe die Gischt der Reuss das Gesicht benetzt und sich ein herrlicher Ausblick auf beide Teufelsbrücken sowie die Trasse der Gotthardbahn bietet.

It pays to take a short break here and wander over the old stone bridge from 1830, through the former military tunnel and up to the Bäzberg viewing platform. Despite the altitude, the spray from the wild Reuss can be felt on the face and the view of the Devil's Bridge and the lines of the Gotthard Railway are spectacular.

---

bergkristallhafte, von Miller & Maranta meisterhaft renovierten Hospiz. Wer nicht in der Albergo San Gottardo gegenüber einkehren möchte, findet an der Passhöhe natürlich die obligatorische Bratwurst, aber auch einen Stand mit exzellenten Tessiner Spezialitäten wie Ziegenkäse und Salami.

Vor der Weiterfahrt muss man sich nun entscheiden: Das einprägsamste Erlebnis ist es, zwischen Sust und Hospiz der alten gepflasterten Tremolastraße zu folgen, die sich auf 4,5 Kilometer Länge in 24 Spitzkehren durch die dramatische Schlucht mehr als 300 Meter hinab ins Tal windet. Die »Tremola« gilt als längstes Straßenbaudenkmal der Schweiz, und die Fahrt über die alten Pflastersteine und durch die von einfachen Granitmauern getragenen Kehren vermitteln einen zeitsprungartigen Eindruck davon, wie die Postillons und frühen Automobilisten die Gotthardüberquerung erlebten. Die neue, in den 1960er- und 1970er-Jahren gebaute Tremolastraße mit ihren kunstvollen Brücken, Lawinengalerien und einem langen Tunnel umfährt die alte Tremolastraße weiträumig, bietet aber – wenn nicht wie so oft der Nebel im Tal hängt – großartige Blicke auf die Kehren der alten Straße und die Granitzinnen jenseits des Bedrettotal. Eindrucksvoll ist auch die frei über dem Talhang schwebende, als Viadukt angelegte Fieud-Serpentine des Tessiner Ingenieurs Giovanni Lombardi, dessen Vorschlag sich auch beim Bau des Gotthard-Straßentunnels durchsetzte. Selbst erfahrenen Automobilisten kribbelt es auf der »Tornante di Fieud« kurz im Magen - sie bietet echtes Achterbahnfeeling. Langsam wird die Landschaft dann wieder sanfter, die verstreuten Granitfelsen weichen grünen Matten und Fichtenwäldern. Man passiert die Festung Motta Bartola und erreicht schließlich den kleinen Talort Airolo. Das obere Tessintal, die Leventina, gehört seit mehr als 200 Jahren zur Schweiz – und doch ist die Nähe zu Italien hier in der Architektur, Sprache, Küche und Kultur bereits allerorts zu spüren. Dass der Gotthardpass nicht nur die Zentralalpen überquert, sondern tatsächlich zwei Welten miteinander verbindet – nach dieser Fahrt hat man es endgültig verstanden.

mountain crystal. Those who would rather skip a visit to the Albergo San Gottardo opposite the hospice can find the obligatory sausage at the top of the pass or stop off at the stall offering excellent Ticino specialities such as goat's cheese and salami.

Before continuing, there is a decision to be made: the most memorable experience would be to follow the old stone-paved Tremola Road between the Sust and the hospice, which snakes down 300 metres through 24 hairpins over 4.5 kilometres through the dramatic gorge and into the valley. The Tremola is considered the longest road construction monument in Switzerland, and the drive over the old paving stones and through the granite-wall-supported curves gives travellers an insight into how it must have been for the postilions and early motorists to cross the Gotthard.

The new Tremola Road, built in the 1960s and 1970s, with its skilfully-engineered bridges, avalanche galleries and long tunnel, takes a wide detour around the old Tremola Road, and if the valley is not blanketed in fog, it offers spectacular views over the zigzagging curves of the old road and the granite pinnacles beyond the Bedretto Valley. As impressive is the Tornante di Fieud: a curving viaduct that swings out over the slope of the valley, built by the Ticino engineer Giovanni Lombardi, whose proposal for the construction of the Gotthard Road Tunnel was also adopted. Even the most seasoned motorists get goosebumps on the viaduct, which gives a real rollercoaster feeling. Gradually, the landscape seems to soften again, with granite rocks scattered over green fields and spruce forests. Past the Motta Bartola fortress, travellers finally arrive in the small community of Airolo. The upper Ticino Valley, the Leventina, has been a part of Switzerland for more than 200 years and yet the architecture, language, cuisine and culture still hold traces of nearby Italy. The fact that the Gotthard Pass not only crosses the Central Alps but actually connects two worlds is finally comprehended after this journey.

RODONT E FORTUEI ....

ÒUT SAN CARLO ....

T
TREMOLA

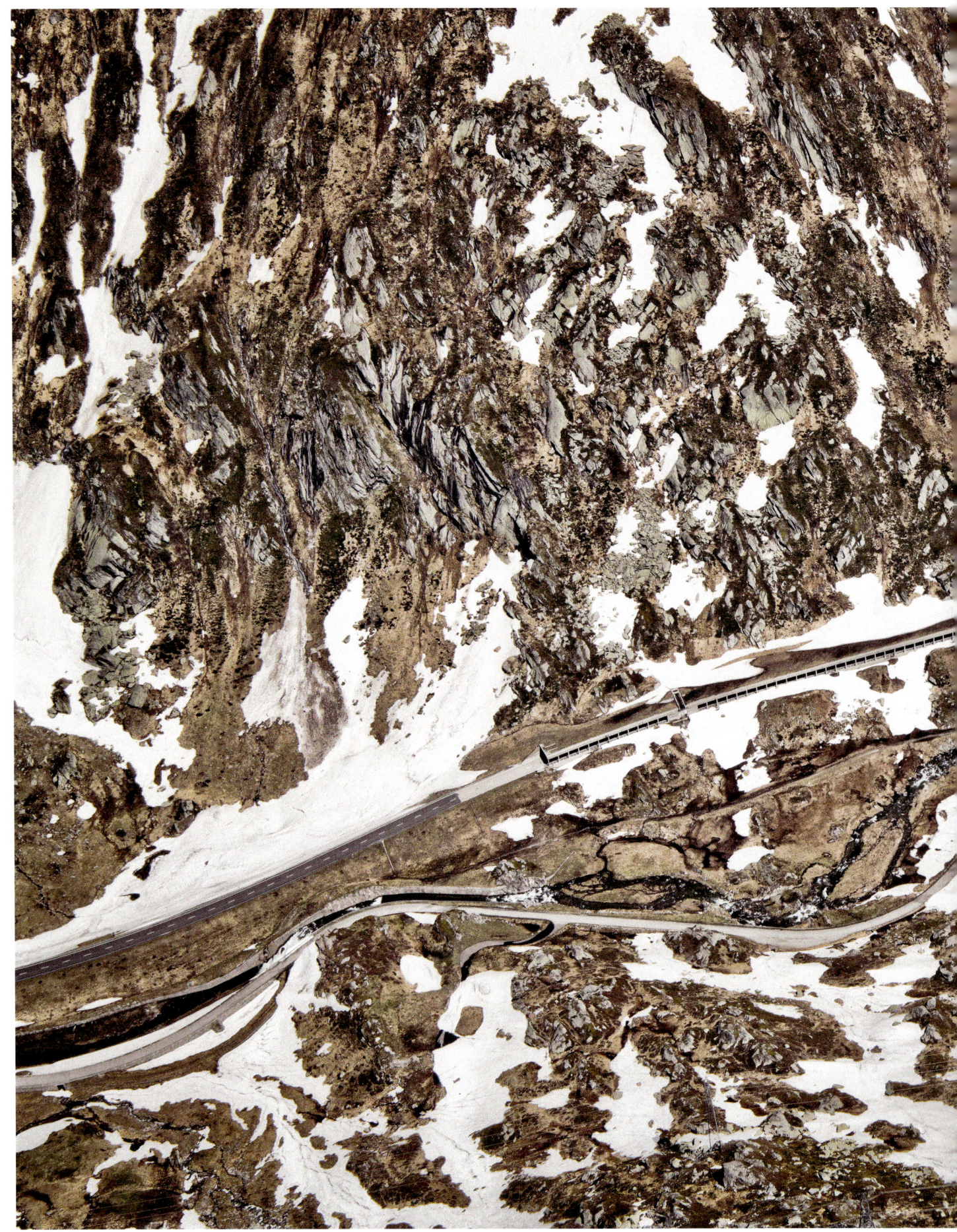

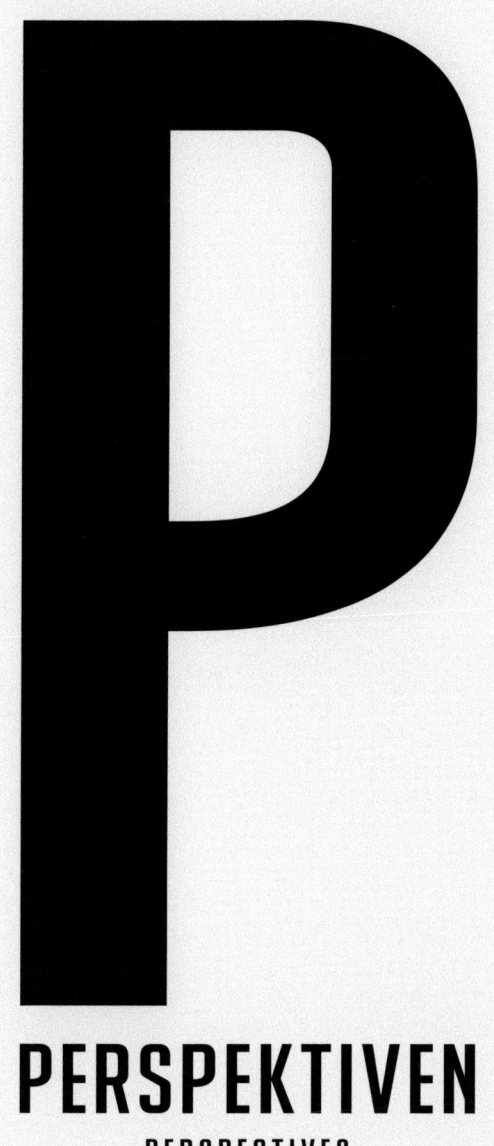

PERSPEKTIVEN
PERSPECTIVES

DIE GROSSE PASSRUNDFAHRT

THE GREAT PASS ROUND TRIP

Der Gotthardpass ist eine der eindrucksvollsten Alpenstraßen Europas. Die Fahrt durch die schroffe Schöllenenschlucht, das weite Hochtal der Urseren oder die Kurven der Tremola gehören zu den spannendsten Bergstrecken, die man mit dem Rennvelo, dem Motorrad oder dem Automobil erfahren kann. Und doch ist die Strecke zwischen Göschenen im Norden und Airolo im Süden nur ein kleiner Teil jener weltweit einzigartigen Passlandschaft, die man rund um das Gotthardmassiv finden kann.

Für die große Passrundfahrt – unseren Kurvenklassiker von rund 220 Kilometern Strecke, den man mit dem Auto oder Motorrad an einem Tag schaffen kann – mieten wir uns unter der Woche im herrlich nostalgischen Gasthaus Sonne in Andermatt ein und starten in aller Herrgottsfrühe via Hospental und Realp in Richtung der wunderbaren Furka-Passstraße, die 1866 eröffnet wurde und auf der sich bereits Sean Connery in seiner Rolle als James Bond im legendären 007-Film Goldfinger zum Kurvenschneiden verleiten ließ. Statt gleich die Metallklingen auszufahren, fahren wir in den scharf geschnittenen Kurven und Kehren erst einmal die Reifen warm und machen dann an der Passhöhe auf 2.431 Metern kurz Halt, um die grandiose Aussicht nach Nordosten ins Urserental und nach Western auf die Berner und Waliser Alpen zu genießen. Auf der Weiterfahrt schießen wir noch schnell das obligatorische Foto in der Kehre vor dem herrlich nostalgischen Hotel Belvédère – das direkt aus einem Wes-Anderson-

The Gotthard Pass is one of the most impressive Alpine roads in Europe. The journey through the steep and craggy Schöllenen Gorge, the open meadows of the high Ursern Valley plateau, or the writhing corners of the Tremola belong to the most thrilling mountain routes which can be experienced on a racing bike, a motorbike or at the wheel of a car. Yet, the stretch between Göschenen in the north and Airolo in the south is just a small part of the unique pass landscape that can be discovered around the Gotthard massif.

We check into the wonderfully nostalgic Gasthaus Sonne in Andermatt, from where we will start our great round trip, a curving classic over a distance of around 220 kilometres, which can be done in one day by car or motorbike. The next morning at the crack of dawn we head off via Hospental and Realp towards the stunning Furka Pass, which was opened in 1866 and became immortalised by Sean Connery's corner-cutting antics in the role of James Bond in the legendary 007 movie Goldfinger. Instead of deploying tyre-slashing hubcap blades, we negotiate the tight, sweeping curves until the tyres are warm and then stop at the top of the pass at 2,431 metres to take in the magnificent vista to the northeast into the Ursern Valley, and to the Bernese and the Pennine Alps in the west. Continuing on, we take a quick obligatory photo of the hairpin in front of the delightfully old-world Hotel Belvédère, which seems to have come straight out of a Wes Anderson movie, before we reach the once elegant hamlet of Gletsch

FURKAPASS

FURKAPASS

GRIMSELPASS

SUSTENPASS

GRIMSELPASS

Film zu stammen scheint –, bevor wir entlang des stetig schmelzenden Rhonegletschers den einst mondänen Talort Gletsch erreichen.

Nicht nur die Pneus, auch unser treuer Boxermotor im Heck hat inzwischen seine Betriebstemperatur erreicht, und so geht es von Goms aus direkt weiter auf die berühmte Grimselpassstraße, die das Berner Oberland mit dem Oberwallis verbindet und an der Passhöhe stolze 2.165 Meter Höhe erreicht. Schon in der Römerzeit war die Passage bekannt, ab dem 12. Jahrhundert existierte am Saumpfad wohl ein Hospiz für Händler und Pilger. 1932 wurde das Tal jedoch geflutet, die Passstraße verlegt und ein gewaltiger Stausee angelegt. Oberhalb der 42 Meter hohen Staumauer thront seitdem das Grimsel Hospiz – ein alpines Viersternehotel auf fast 2.000 Meter Höhe mit wunderbarem Blick auf den Zinkenstock, das Finsteraarhorn und den See. Doch für eine Einkehr in dem exzellent bestückten Felsenweinkeller ist es wirklich noch zu früh. Viel lieber folgen wir der herrlichen Topografie der Straße durch scharfe S-Kurven und dunkle Tunnels, über Gebirgsbäche und entlang schwarzer Felsen, spielen mit Kupplung und Bremse, lassen uns vom Dröhnen und Bellen des Motors den Takt vorgeben, bis sich das Tal öffnet und wir zuerst das Örtchen Guttannen und schließlich Innertkirchen erreichen.

Von hier aus lohnt ein Abstecher in die dramatische Aareschlucht oder zu den Reichenbachfällen, wo einst Sherlock Holmes im Kampf mit seinem Erzfeind Professor Moriarty in die Tiefe stürzte. Doch unsere Zeit ist knapp bemessen, und wir folgen unserem Kurvenhunger weiter nach Osten auf den Sustenpass. Zwischen den 1930er- und 1950er-Jahren ausgebaut, gilt der Sustenpass in seiner heutigen Form als modernes schweizerisches Architekturdenkmal und Musterstück der Straßenbaukunst. Das architektonische Spiel mit der Topografie beschert uns hier eine rasant geschnittene Folge von Durchblicken, Tiefblicken, Hochblicken, Überblicken, Voraus- und Rückblicken – ein geradezu filmisches Wahrnehmungserlebnis! Von der Passhöhe auf 2.224 Metern geht es schließlich in großzügigen Serpentinen durchs Maiental hinab nach Wassen im Urnerland. Zurück auf der Gotthardstraße, folgen wir dem dramatischsten Teil der Strecke durch Tunnels, Galerien, Serpentinen und die enge Schöllenenschlucht hinauf ins Urserental und weiter zur Passhöhe, wo wir uns mit einer auf offenem Feuer gegrillten Kalbsbratwurst belohnen.

Doch der Sechszylinder knistert und knackt unternehmungslustig, und so geht es nach kurzer Pause schon wieder hinab in die Leventina – natürlich über die ehrwürdigen Pflastersteine der Tremola. Nirgends ist der alte Geist der Gotthardstraße so lebendig wie hier! In Airolo angekommen, biegen wir schließlich nach Westen ab und folgen dem Bedrettotal, bis sich die Straße

along the constantly melting Rhône Glacier. By now, the tyres as well as our trusty boxer engine in the rear have reached the perfect operating temperature, and we push on from Goms directly to the famous Grimsel Pass Road, which links the Bernese Oberland with the Upper Valais, reaching the top of the pass at an impressive altitude of 2,165 metres. The Romans already knew about this passage, on which a bridle path and very likely a hospice existed for traders and pilgrims from the 12th century. In 1932, however, a massive reservoir was built, the valley was submerged and the pass road was relocated. Above the 42-metre-high dam wall sits the Grimsel Hospice; a four-star Alpine hotel at an elevation of almost 2,000 metres with spectacular views of the Zinkenstock, the Finsteraarhorn and the lake. Unfortunately, it's too early in the day to sample the wonderful wines stored in the rustic rock-walled cellar. We choose to follow the glorious topography of the road through the sharp esses and dark tunnels, over mountain streams and along black rock walls; playing with the clutch and brakes and allowing the hum and the roar of the engine to dictate the rhythm until the valley opens up before us and we reach the village of Guttannen and then Innertkirchen.

From here, it's worth taking a detour to the dramatic Aare Gorge or the Reichenbach Falls, where Sherlock Holmes and his arch enemy Professor Moriarty were allegedly locked in mortal combat. We don't have much time, so we quench our thirst for serpentines further to the east at the Susten Pass. Constructed between the 1930s and 1950s, the Susten Pass of today is regarded as a Swiss architectural monument and masterpiece of road construction. The architectural play with the topography provides constantly changing views: downwards, upwards, wide-angle, telephoto and everything in between – a veritable cinematic extravaganza! From the pass summit at 2,224 metres, we snake our way down generous switchbacks through Maiental to Wassen in the canton of Uri. Back on the Gotthard Road, we follow the most dramatic part of the route through tunnels, galleries, serpentines and the narrow Schöllenen Gorge up to the Ursern Valley and on to the top of the pass, where we fortify ourselves with veal sausages grilled on an open fire.

But the crackles and clicks of the six-cylinder lure us back to our adventure, and after a short break, we weave our way down again into the Leventina, over the venerable paving stones of the Tremola, of course. Nowhere is the old spirit of the Gotthard Road as alive as it is here! Arriving in Airolo, we turn to the west and follow the Bedretto Valley until the road begins its ascent to the Nufenen Pass. At 2,478 metres, it is still the highest Alpine pass in Switzerland, and even in early summer, travellers should check whether it is closed due to late snowfall. The 37-kilometre-long high-alpine section between the Bedretto Valley in Ticino and Ulrichen in the

Auf der finalen Fahrt über die Furka tanzen wir schließlich den letzten Serpentinentango und staunen nochmals darüber, wie unterschiedlich sich ein- und dieselbe Passstraße doch anfühlen kann, wenn man sie in entgegengesetzter Richtung befährt.

schließlich hinauf zum Nufenenpass zu winden beginnt. Mit 2.478 Metern ist er bis heute der höchstgelegene Alpenpass der Schweiz – und so sollte man sich auch im Frühsommer noch versichern, ob die Strecke nicht wegen anhaltenden Schneefalls gesperrt ist. Die 37 Kilometer lange, hochalpine Straße zwischen dem Tessiner Bedrettotal und Ulrichen im Goms wurde erst 1969 eröffnet und gilt unter Kurvenliebhabern als Geheimtipp. Hinauf geht es auf einfachen Betonplatten und sofern Wind und Wetter es zulassen, bietet sich an der Passhöhe ein atemberaubender Blick auf die Berner Alpen im Norden und den Griesgletscher im Süden.

Doch noch ist der Kurvenhunger nicht gestillt. Auf kunstvollen Kehren schwingen wir uns hinab ins wilde Aeginental. Wir überqueren die Rhone und erreichen zum zweiten Mal an diesem Tag das Dörfchen Gletsch. Auf der finalen Fahrt über die Furka tanzen wir schließlich den letzten Serpentinentango und staunen nochmals darüber, wie unterschiedlich sich ein- und dieselbe Passstraße doch anfühlen kann, wenn man sie in entgegengesetzter Richtung befährt. Dann ist es jedoch wirklich an der Zeit, das geschätzte Kurvensportgerät mit seinen heißgebremsten Eisen in die Nachtruhe zu verabschieden, die Passrundfahrt bei einer ordentlichen Portion Rösti mit Spiegeleiern und einem Glas Blauburgunder in der Stube der Sonne nochmals Revue passieren zu lassen – und anschließend mit seligem Lächeln in einen tiefen und traumlosen Schlaf zu fallen.

On the final stretch over the Furka, we dance our final serpentine tango and are amazed once again at how different a pass road can look when driven in the opposite direction.

canton of Valais, was only opened in 1969 and is an insider's tip for cornering connoisseurs. Winding upwards over simple concrete slabs, and if wind and weather allow, the top of the pass offers a breathtaking view of the Bernese Alps to the north and the Gries Glacier in the south.

But still the hunger for curves is not satiated. Twisting and turning, we sweep our way down into the wild Aeginen Valley and cross the Rhône to arrive in the village of Gletsch for the second time in one day. On the final stretch over the Furka, we dance our final serpentine tango and are amazed once again at how different a pass road can look when driven in the opposite direction. By now, it is high time to say goodnight to our beloved cornering sports equipment with its hot brakes, and relive our round trip with a hearty serving of potato rösti with fried eggs and a glass of Pinot Noir in the quaint dining room of the Sonne Hotel, and finally, with a blissful smile, fall into a deep and dreamless sleep.

DAS HOSPIZ AM GOTTHARDPASS

THE HOSPICE AT THE GOTTHARD PASS

Man kann die Straße über den Sankt Gotthard und die Gebäude an der Passhöhe anthropologisch-abstrakt als Spuren menschlicher Kultur und ihrer Auseinandersetzung mit der Umwelt betrachten – für die einstigen Baumeister und ihre Zeitgenossen ging es hingegen um viel mehr; entschieden doch die Bauten nicht selten über Leben und Tod. Jede neue Brücke, jeder Tunnel und jede Lawinengalerie machten die Reise über den Pass etwas weniger riskant. Kein Gebäude am Gotthard steht derart sinnbildlich für die Gefahren der hochalpinen Landschaft und ihre Überwindung durch Baukunst und menschliche Gastfreundschaft wie das alte Hospiz, das Vecchio Ospizio San Gottardo.

Schon zu karolingischer Zeit, zwischen dem 7. und 9. Jahrhundert, fand sich an der Passhöhe des Gotthards eine kleine Kapelle, in der man um göttlichen Schutz und Beistand bitten konnte. Zwischen 1166 und 1176, also wahrscheinlich noch vor der Öffnung der Schöllenenschlucht, wurde das Gotteshaus erweitert und im Jahr 1230 schließlich durch den Mailänder Erzbischof Enrico Settala dem heiligen Sankt Godehard von Hildesheim geweiht. Schon sieben Jahre später, der Handelsverkehr zwischen Uri und Tessin war da bereits fest etabliert, war in den Säumerstatuten des Dorfes Osco in der Leventina erstmals von einem Hospiz am Pass die Rede. Das Gebäude nahe der Kapelle wurde wahrscheinlich von Geistlichen betrieben und bot vor allem Pilgerreisenden Schutz vor Wind und Wetter, Schnee und Lawinen. Arme Leute erhielten umsonst Kost und Logis und wurden im Krankheitsfall gepflegt, bis sie wieder weiterreisen konnten. Aber auch Händler konnten im Hospiz unterkommen – für sie standen Warenlager, Stallungen und Gästezimmer bereit.

Das Bild des Hospizwirtes, der hoch oben am Pass bei Nacht und Nebel oder im Schneetreiben nach verlorenen Reisenden leuchtet, mag uns heute romantische Schauer über den Rücken jagen – doch in den ersten Jahrhunderten des Gotthard-Saumhandels waren die Schrecken der Bergwelt äußerst real und alles anderes als romantisch. Davon zeugte auch die Totenkapelle am Rande der Tremolaschlucht: Die leblosen Körper namenloser, erfrorener, von Steinen erschlagener oder von Seuchen dahingeraffter Reisenden wurden in dem offenen Gebäude verwahrt, bis das Bergklima und die lokalen Bären, Wölfe und Luchse ihren Teil erledigt hatten und die Gebeine

From an anthropological point of view, one can consider the road over the Saint Gotthard and the buildings at the top of the pass as traces of human culture and their confrontation with the environment. For the early builders and their contemporaries, however, it was much more: the structures often meant the difference between life and death. Every new bridge, every tunnel and every avalanche gallery made the journey across the pass a little less risky. No building on the Gotthard epitomises the dangers of the high alpine landscapes and the conquest of these hazards through the building skill and human hospitality more so than the Old Hospice, the Vecchio Ospizio San Gottardo.

As early as the Carolingian period between the 7th and 9th centuries, a small chapel stood at the top of the Gotthard where one could pray for divine protection and assistance. Between 1166 and 1176, probably before the opening of the Schöllenen Gorge, this chapel was extended and, in the year 1230, the Archbishop of Milan, Enrico de Settala finally dedicated this building to Saint Godehard of Hildesheim. Seven years later, when trade between Uri and Ticino had become firmly established, the mule transport statutes of the town of Osco in the Leventina first mentioned a hospice at the pass. The building near the chapel was probably run by clerics and offered pilgrims protection from wind and weather, snow and avalanches. The poor received free food and lodging and, if ill, were tended to until they were well enough to continue. Traders, too, stayed at the hospice where there were storage areas, stables and guest rooms.

The image of the hospice host who takes his torch out in foggy nights or in blizzards to search for lost travellers may evoke a romantic thrill in us today, but during the first centuries of the Gotthard hauling trade, the horrors of the mountain world were very real and anything but romantic. The Chapel of the Dead at the precipice of the Tremola Gorge is also testimony to this: the lifeless bodies of nameless casualties, frozen to death, killed by falling rocks or disease, were laid in an open structure until the mountain climate and the bears, wolves and lynxes had done their part, and the bones fell through holes in the wall and into the abyss. For those running the hospice, life was not easy either. Huge amounts of firewood and food for the guests were needed, as well as hay and straw for the pack animals. Almost everything had to be

durch ein Loch im Gemäuer in die Tiefe fielen. Auch für die Hospizwirte war das Leben beschwerlich: Man benötigte gewaltige Mengen an Brennholz sowie Lebensmittel für die Gäste sowie Heu und Stroh für die Saumtiere. Fast alles musste aus dem Tal mühsam heraufgetragen werden. Zudem wurden das Hospiz und seine Nebengebäude immer wieder beschädigt oder ganz zerstört – mal von Lawinen, mal von marodierenden Soldaten – und den Anforderungen der Zeit entsprechend neu aufgebaut.

Die Kapuzinermönche nahmen jährlich oft mehr als 4.000 Reisende auf. Für den Unterhalt kamen die Gemeinden auf – die Mittel stammten meist aus Sustrechten und Einkünften aus dem Gütertransport. Mit der Zunahme des Saumverkehrs traten säkulare Gastwirte anstelle der Geistlichen. Auch das Gästeprofil des Gotthardhospizes änderte sich: Zu den illustren Zeitgenossen, die ihrer Alpensehnsucht bis auf die Passhöhe folgten, gehörten Horace Bénédict de Saussure, Johann Wolfgang von Goethe und Honoré de Balzac, später auch Giuseppe Maria Garibaldi, Felix Mendelssohn Bartholdy und Arthur Rimbaud. Im Jahr 1841 wurde die Führung des Hospizes dem Tessiner Transitinspektor Felice Lombardi übertragen. Sein Sohn errichtete 1863 – zur Blütezeit des Schweizerischen Alpentourismus – ein neues Hotel namens Monte Prosa und erwarb auch bald die Sust, das Hospiz und die Kapelle. Doch mit der Eröffnung der Gotthardbahn im Jahr 1882 verloren die Bauten an der Passhöhe für die Reisenden ihre lebenswichtige Bedeutung – die größte Gefahr einer Gotthardpassage war es nun, sich im rüttelnden Halbdunkel des Salonwagen während der Tunnelfahrt auf den Gehrock zu aschen. Dennoch hielt die Familie Lombardi an ihren Gotthardbauten fest; ja, mehr noch: Nach einem Feuer im Jahr 1905 wurde das Hospiz sogar neu aufgebaut – dieses Mal ohne seine Holzverkleidung und mit steilem Satteldach.

Erst Anfang der 1970er Jahre – nach 130 Jahren im Familienbesitz – entschied sich ein betagter Lombardi-Erbe zum Verkauf. Da sich kein Käufer fand, entschied er sich für eine List: Er setzte sich in den Zug nach Norden, schaltete in der Frankfurter Allgemeinen Zeitung ein großes Inserat, kaufte so viele Zeitungen, wie er tragen konnte und fuhr zurück zum Gotthard, um die Druckwaren zu verteilen. Aufgeschreckt von der Vorstellung, deutsche Großinvestoren könnten sich den symbolträchtigen Ort eidgenössischer Geschichte und Unabhängigkeit einverleiben, schritt der Schweizerische Heimatschutz zur Tat, gründete die Stiftung Pro San Gottardo und sammelte flugs die Finanzmittel ein, um die Gebäude am Pass zu übernehmen. Das Hotel Monte Prosa wurde in San Gottardo umbenannt, die Kapelle restauriert, in der Alten Sust ein Museum eröffnet.

Im Jahr 2006 wurde die Renovierung des Alten Hospizes in Angriff genommen. Den Wettbewerb konnte das Basler Architekturbüro Miller & Maranta, das bereits das legendäre Hotel Waldhaus in Sils-Maria mit viel Fein-

laboriously lugged from the valley. What's more, the hospice and the outbuildings were constantly damaged or completely destroyed by avalanches or even marauding soldiers and rebuilt according to the requirements of the time.

It was not uncommon for the Capuchin monks to welcome more than 4,000 visitors each year. The communities took care of the upkeep, mostly from Sust dues and income from the transport of goods. With the increase in goods traffic, secular innkeepers replaced the clergy. The type of guest at the Gotthard also changed: among the illustrious contemporaries who followed their alpine yearning to the top of the pass were Horace Bénédict de Saussure, Johann Wolfgang von Goethe and Honoré de Balzac, and later Giuseppe Maria Garibaldi, Felix Mendelssohn and Arthur Rimbaud.

In 1841, the management of the hospice was taken over by the Ticino transit inspector Felice Lombardi. His son built a new hotel called Monte Prosa in 1863 – during the heyday of Swiss Alpine tourism – and soon also acquired the Sust, the hospice and the chapel. However, with the opening of the Gotthard Railway in 1882, the buildings at the pass lost their importance to travellers. Now, the greatest danger when crossing the Gotthard was for travellers to drop cigar ash on their frock coats as the wagon rattled through the dim tunnel. Nevertheless, the Lombardi family held on to their Gotthard buildings. Indeed, after a fire in 1905, the hospice was even rebuilt, this time without its wood panelling and with a steep gabled roof.

Only in the early 1970s, after 130 years of family ownership, did an elderly Lombardi heir decide to sell. Finding no buyer interest, he came up with a cunning plan: he caught a train to the north, took out a big advertisement in the Frankfurter Allgemeine Zeitung, bought as many as he could carry and took the newspapers back to the Gotthard to distribute. Alarmed by the idea that major German investors could purchase an historic piece of Swiss history and independence, the Swiss Homeland Security Commission leapt into action, founded the Pro San Gottardo Foundation and quickly raised funds to take over the buildings at the pass. The Monte Prosa Hotel was renamed the San Gottardo, the chapel was restored, and a museum was opened in the old warehouse.

In 2006, renovation work on the Old Hospice began. The contract was awarded to the Basel-based architectural firm Miller & Maranta, which had already upgraded the legendary Hotel Waldhaus in Sils-Maria with great sensitivity. The design veered away from the nostalgic alpine cliché as well as bold modernity. Instead, the architects decided on an 'evolutionary' modernisation to the hospice, in keeping with the century-long ongoing changes and rebuilds. Thus, between 2008 and 2010, an understated yet monumental building was created that blended seamlessly into the harsh environment, yet still

322 — DAS HOSPIZ / THE HOSPICE

gefühl modernisiert hatte, für sich entscheiden. Der Entwurf verzichtete auf nostalgisch-alpine Klischees wie auf plakative Modernität. Vielmehr hatten sich die Architekten dazu entschlossen, das im Laufe der Jahrhunderte immer wieder veränderte und neu errichtete Hospiz im Rahmen einer evolutionären Modernisierung »weiterzubauen«. So entstand zwischen 2008 und 2010 ein ebenso schlichtes wie monumentales Gebäude, das sich nahtlos in die raue Umgebung einfügt – und dennoch an der Passhöhe einen beeindruckenden visuellen Akzent setzt. Die Kapelle wurde in das Gesamtvolumen des Gebäudes integriert, mit Maueraufsätzen aus Beton ein zusätzliches Stockwerk auf die Bruchsteinwand aufgesetzt, nach Norden das Dach tief heruntergezogen und mit Bleiplatten verkleidet, nach Süden die Giebelwand in die Höhe gestreckt.

Wirkt das polygonale, massive, nur von kleinen Fensterschachten durchbrochene Gebäude von außen beinahe so abweisend wie der Gotthard selbst, wurde das Innere des Hospizes derart gestaltet, dass die Gäste sich auch bei Sturm und Schnee rundum sicher und geborgen fühlen. Da die Bauzeit im Gebirge begrenzt ist, wurden die Verkleidungen der Zimmer im Tal aus unbehandeltem Fichtenholz vorkonstruiert und anschließend am Berg in die feste Mauerhülle eingesetzt. Während der Duft des Holzes den gesamten Raum bestimmt, ist die Möblierung betont zurückhaltend: Ein einfaches Bett, ein Bugholzstuhl von Thonet, ein von Miller & Maranta entworfener Sekretär – nichts soll von der alpinen Erfahrung und dem Blick aus dem Fenster auf die schroffe Gebirgswelt ablenken. Auch in der Stube, die als Gemeinschaftsraum dient, und dem benachbarten Lesezimmer wurden ein alter Specksteinofen, schlichte Holzmöbel und einige Designklassiker von Hans J. Wegner und Poul Henningsen so zurückhaltend kombiniert, dass sich der Herzschlag beim Betreten augenblicklich verlangsamt und man nach wenigen Augenblicken zur Ruhe kommt. Wer auf opulenten Luxus verzichten kann und in den Höhen der Schweizer Alpen einen minimalistischen Ort der Einkehr sucht, findet im Vecchio Ospizio San Gottardo von Miller & Maranta vor allem in der Neben- und Nebelsaison im Mai, September und Oktober sicherlich sein Glück.

Dass der Gotthard auch fast zwei Jahrhunderte nach dem Ende das Saumhandels für ein Schreckensschauspiel gut ist, zeigte sich auch uns während einer Recherchereise: Eine ganze Nacht lang blitzte und donnerte es um die Passhöhe und das Alte Hospiz herum so markerschütternd und brachial, als hätten die Götter des alt-eidgenössischen Olymps zu einer kosmischen Techno-Party geladen. Wir konnten freilich nicht anders, als das Schauspiel in dicke Daunendecken gehüllt an unseren Fenstern zu verfolgen und unwillkürlich all jener Händler, Pilger und Reisenden zu gedenken, die einst im Flackern der Blitze ihren Weg durch die nachtschwarze Felslandschaft suchten, bis sie in der Ferne endlich die rettende Laterne des Hospizwirtes erspähten.

presented an impressive visual highlight at the top of the pass. The chapel was integrated into the overall complex, with an additional floor added to the quarry stone outer wall anchored by concrete elements. The steeply sloping roof on the northern side was extended down, and clad with lead panels, with the south-facing gabled facade stretching skywards.

If, from the outside, the massive, polygonal shape broken only by small windows seems almost as uninviting as the Gotthard itself, the interior of the hospice has been designed in such a way that guests feel safe and secure even in blizzards and snow. Since construction time in the mountains is limited, the cladding for the rooms was prefabricated out of untreated spruce wood down in the valley and transported up the mountain and fitted into the solid masonry. While the scent from the wood permeates the entire room, the furnishings are minimalistic: a simple bed, a Thonet bentwood chair, a tallboy designed by Miller & Maranta. The idea is that nothing should distract from the alpine experience and the view from the window to the rugged mountainscape. And in the parlour, which also serves as a lounge, and the adjacent reading room, an old soapstone stove, simple wooden furniture and some design classics from Hans J. Wegner and Poul Henningsen come together in such an uncluttered way that upon entering the space, one immediately slows down and relaxes. If you can do without opulent luxury and are looking for a minimalistic retreat at the roof of the Swiss Alps, you will certainly enjoy spending time at the Miller & Maranta-renovated Ospizio San Gottardo, particularly in the off-peak and shoulder seasons of May, September and October.

Even two centuries after the end of the hauling trade, the Gotthard is still good for a terrifying experience. This is what we found out during our research trip. For the entire night, lightning and thunder boomed and roared with such terrifying intensity around the Old Hospice at the top of the pass, that it felt as if the Gods of the old Swiss Olympus were throwing a cosmic techno party. We could do nothing more than watch the spectacle from our windows, wrapped up warm in thick down duvets, and think of all the traders, pilgrims and travellers who once stumbled their way through the pitch-black and rocky landscape in the flickering flashes of the lightning bolts until they finally spied the comforting lantern of the hospice host in the distance.

PASSO DEL S. GOTTARDO
6780 AIROLO
SVIZZERA
PHONE: +41 91 869 12 35
FAX: +41 91 869 18 11
EMAIL: INFO@PASSOSANGOTTARDO.CH
WWW.PASSOSANGOTTARDO.CH

SASSO SAN GOTTARDO

Die Verteidigung der Alpenpässe und insbesondere des Gotthards nimmt in der Geschichte der Schweiz eine Schlüsselrolle ein. Die alte Eidgenossenschaft entstand im Bündnis der nördlichen Gotthard-Kantone gegen den Zugriff fremder Herrscher und wuchs über die Jahrhunderte entlang der Handelsroute nach Norden und Süden zu seiner heutigen Form. Nachdem zuerst Napoleon und schließlich die Großmächte Europas der jungen Schweiz ihre Neutralität und damit auch die Wacht über ihre strategisch wichtigen Alpenübergänge verordnet hatten, wurde der Schutz des Gotthardpasses Teil der Staatsraison. Mit dem Machtgewinn Deutschlands und Italiens und dem Erfolg der Gotthard-Eisenbahn im späten 19. Jahrhundert entwickelte sich schließlich die Notwendigkeit, die geopolitisch wichtige Alpentraversale auch militärisch zu sichern. Im Süden der Passhöhe entstanden die ersten Wehranlagen. Zur Zitadelle ausgebaut wurde der Gotthard schließlich während des Zweiten Weltkrieges – als Herzstück des »Réduit national« war das mit Bunkern, Tunneln und Schießscharten durchlöcherte Zentralmassiv zum ultimativen Rückzugsort und letzten »Faustpfand« der Schweizer Unabhängigkeit gegen die Übermacht der faschistischen Achsenmächte geworden.

Ein ebenso eindrucksvolles wie verstörendes Zeugnis dieser unsicheren Zeit findet man heute in der Erlebniswelt »Sasso San Gottardo«: Im Zweiten Weltkrieg war die Festung ein wichtiges Glied im alpinen Befestigungswall der Schweiz. Und auch in den Jahrzehnten danach, zur Zeit des Kalten Krieges, wurde die streng geheim gehaltene Anlage weiter unterhalten, von Soldaten bewohnt und bei regelmäßigen Wehrübungen auf ihre sofortige Einsatzbereitschaft überprüft. Erst 1998 wurde der Betrieb eingestellt, im Jahr 2001 – ein gutes Jahrzehnt nach dem Fall des Eisernen Vorhangs – die Festung aus der Geheimhaltung entlassen. 2012 eröffnete in den alten Stollen

Defending the Alpine passes, particularly the Gotthard, played an important role throughout the history of Switzerland. The old Swiss Confederation emerged from the alliance of the northern Gotthard cantons against the grasp of foreign rulers, and developed over the centuries along the trade route to the north and south to its present-day form.

After Napoleon, and later the great powers of Europe, had decreed neutrality to the young Switzerland, and thus also the monitoring of the strategically important Alpine crossings, the protection of the Gotthard Pass became part of the reason of state. In the late 19th century, with Germany and Italy gaining power and the growing success of the Gotthard Railway, it finally became necessary to militarily secure this geopolitically important Alpine transit route. South of the pass, the first fortifications were built and the Gotthard eventually turned into a citadel during the Second World War. At the core of the 'Réduit National', the central massif interspersed with its bunkers, tunnels and embrasures, became the ultimate place of retreat and the last line of defence of Swiss independence against the dominance of the fascist Axis powers.

An impressive and at the same time disturbing testimony to this precarious time can be found today in the 'Sasso San Gottardo' Museum: during the Second World War, this fortress played a critical part in Switzerland's fortified Alpine ramparts. Even in the following decades during the Cold War era, this top-secret facility was manned by soldiers, who regularly took part in military exercises in readiness for immediate deployment. The operation only closed down in 1998. In 2001, a good decade after the fall of the Iron Curtain, the Swiss government declassified the fortress and, in 2012,

GOTTHARD · PORSCHE DRIVE

SASSO SAN GOTTARDO — 325

schließlich das Museum »Sasso San Gottardo«. Nur wenige Gehminuten von den Wurst- und Souvenirständen der Passhöhe entfernt, führt unter Urner, Schweizer und Tessiner Flagge ein unscheinbarer Tunnel in die Felswand. Folgt man dem düsteren Schacht weiter in den Berg, erreicht man schließlich eine Cafeteria, an der sich die Wege gabeln – und man unwillkürlich und fröstelnd realisiert, im Zentrum einer unterirdischen Stadt angelangt zu sein. Als eines von 73 Schweizerischen Artilleriewerken im Rahmen der Réduit-Strategie geplant, wurde die Festung »Sasso da Pigna« zwischen 1941 und 1945 gebaut. Im Herbst 1944 waren die vier Bunkerkanonen sowie der gesamte Fortabschnitt mit den Kampfstellungen einsatzbereit. Die Fertigstellung erfolgte im Dezember 1945 – ein halbes Jahr nach Ende des Krieges.

Folgt man den Gängen einige Kilometer weiter in den Berg und fährt mit dem Schrägaufzug »Metro del Sasso« – den die Soldaten jedoch nicht selbst benutzen durften – durch einen weiteren Tunnel, gelangt man in den eigentlichen Teil der Festung »Sasso da Pigna«. Die Unterkünfte im Inneren boten Platz für rund 420 Soldaten, die in bedrückenden Mannschaftsräumen kartenspielend auf ihre Schicht warteten, am einzigen Fernsprecher mit ihren Freundinnen im Flachland telefonierten oder die Munition durch die engen Verbindungstunnel schleppten. Tatsächlich wirkt es, als sei die Festung eben erst verlassen worden – in den Schlafsälen scheint sogar der Duft nasser Männersocken noch in der Luft zu hängen. Der wahre Schrecken der Anlage eröffnet sich allerdings in den Geschützständen und Munitionsmagazinen: Während die Soldaten hier aus dem Dunkel ihrer Felsenfestung nach Kräften gefeuert und die karge Berglandschaft verteidigt hätten, wäre bei einem Überfall der deutschen Armee das Schweizer Mittelland praktisch kampflos in die Hände der nationalsozialistischen Besatzer gefallen – und mit ihm die meisten Eltern, Frauen und Kinder der Gotthardsoldaten. Max Frisch, der zwischen 1939 und 1943 selbst als Kanonier Dienst am Gotthard geleistet hatte, bezeichnete die aus der Not heraus entstandene Réduit-Strategie später kritisch als »Verteidigung der Murmeltiere«.

Wer nach den bedrückenden Impressionen mentale Erleichterung sucht, findet in der »Erlebniswelt Gotthard« erbaulichere Exponate wie etwa eine Ausstellung atemberaubender Riesenkristalle aus dem Gotthardmassiv. Dennoch ist man erleichtert, wenn man nach zwei Stunden im Inneren des Berges wieder aus dem Tunnel tritt, frische Luft atmen und in den freien Himmel hinaufblicken kann. Kaum vorstellbar, dass die Festungssoldaten mitunter mehrere Monate im Dunkel der Gotthardzitadelle verbringen mussten. Nicht nur Kriegstreibern und Militaristen sei der Besuch des »Sasso San Gottardo« dennoch wärmstens empfohlen – als abschreckendes Beispiel und Erinnerung daran, wie fragil und wenig selbstverständlich unser Frieden in Europa doch sein kann und dass Krieg mit Menschen geführt wird, und nicht mit abstrakten Maschinen.

the old caverns were opened to the public as the Sasso San Gottardo Museum.

Within easy walking distance of the sausage and souvenir stands at the pass summit, an inconspicuous tunnel leads into the rock face under Uri, Swiss and Ticino flags. Following the gloomy shafts deeper into the mountain, visitors finally come to a cafeteria where the path forks – and they suddenly realise with a shiver that they have reached the centre of an underground city. Planned as one of the 73 Swiss artillery fortresses as part of the Redoubt strategy, the 'Sasso da Pigna' fortress was built between 1941 and 1945. By autumn 1944, four bunker cannons and the entire fort passage were geared up for combat. In December 1945, six months after the end of the war, the fortress was finally completed.

Walking a few kilometres along the corridors into the mountain and then taking the 'Metro del Sasso' underground cable car, which soldiers were not permitted to use, another tunnel leads to the actual part of the 'Sasso da Pigna' fortress. Inside, there was room to accommodate 420 soldiers, who played cards in claustrophobic quarters while waiting for their shift to start, phoned their girlfriends in the lowlands on the only telephone, or dragged ammunition through the narrow connecting tunnels. One is left with the feeling that the troops have only just left the fortress.

In the dormitories the smell of damp socks still seems to hang in the air. The real horror of the facility, however, is found in the artillery stands and ammunition magazines: the atmosphere evokes the image of soldiers firing from the darkness of their rock fortress to defend the barren mountain landscape, while Central Switzerland surrenders virtually without a fight to the German army, and falls into the hands of the Nazi occupiers – among them the parents, wives and children of the Gotthard soldiers. Max Frisch, who had served as a gunner at the Gotthard between 1939 and 1943, later criticised the Redoubt strategy, which had emerged as a necessary measure, as the 'defence of the marmots'.

Those who are looking for some mental relief after such dark impressions can find more uplifting exhibits in the 'Gotthard World of Experiences', including breathtaking giant crystals from the Gotthard massif. As impressive as it is, after two hours in the bowels of the mountain, it is a relief to emerge into the fresh air outside and gaze up into open skies. It is hard to imagine that the soldiers in this fortress sometimes had to spend several months in the darkness of the Gotthard citadel. Still, a visit to the 'Sasso San Gottardo' is not only for warmongers and militarists; it also serves as a reminder and deterrent of just how fragile peace can be in Europe and is something not to be taken for granted. After all, war is waged with people and not with abstract machines.

DRIVE

Die Geschichte des Gotthardpasses ist auch eine Entwicklungsgeschichte der menschlichen Mobilität. In den ersten Jahrhunderten nach der Öffnung der Schöllenenschlucht um das Jahr 1200 herum waren die Händler und Pilger, die den Gotthardpass überquerten, meist noch zu Fuß unterwegs. Im Zuge der Professionalisierung des Saumhandels wurde der Pfad immer weiter ausgebaut und Stück für Stück für Pferde und Ochsen passierbar gemacht. Mit dem Bau der ersten Fahrstraße über den Gotthard begann ab 1830 schließlich das Zeitalter der Postkutschen – das allerdings schon im Jahr 1882 wieder endete, als die Gotthardbahn ihren Betrieb durch den neuen Tunnel aufnahm. Im frühen 20. Jahrhundert erschienen die ersten Automobilisten auf dem Pass, die Straße wurde weiter ausgebaut. Mit dem Boom des Individualverkehrs und Massentourismus fand die Gotthardstraße in der Nachkriegszeit schließlich zu ihrer heutigen Form, bis 1980 der erste Straßentunnel durchs Gotthardmassiv die einst beschwerliche, viele Tage in Anspruch nehmende Reise durch die Alpen auf eine 15-minütige Fahrt verkürzte.

Auf dem Sattel eines Velos, eines Motorrads oder am Steuer eines Automobils kann man den Gotthard deshalb auch als gewaltiges Freilichtmuseum erfahren – ein mehr als 800 Jahre alten Kulturbau, dessen Pfade sich einst an die alpine Topografie schmiegten und dessen Streckenführung über die Jahrhunderte immer mehr dem Ideal der schnellsten und kürzesten Verbindung, der Luftlinie, angenähert wurde. Wir mögen die Teufelsbrücke und die Kurven der Tremola bewundern und in Nostalgie den alten Zeiten nachhängen, als eine Passfahrt noch ein Erlebnis war. Doch historisch betrachtet, hatten auch die schönsten Brücken und sinnlichsten Serpentinen stets nur ein Ziel: Die Reisezeit zwischen Nord und Süd zu verkürzen, die Fahrt schneller, sicherer und bequemer zu machen.

Es entbehrt nicht einer gewissen Ironie, dass wir – die wir der maximalen Beschleunigung so nahe gekommen sind – nun genau diese alten Straßen heimsuchen, um die Fahrzeit am Steuer unserer Rennräder und hart gefederten Sportwagen wieder künstlich in die Länge zu zie-

The history of the Gotthard Pass also tells the story of human mobility. In the first centuries after the Schöllenen Gorge opened, around the year 1200, traders and pilgrims still crossed the Gotthard Pass mostly on foot. As part of the professionalisation of the pack-mule trade, the bridle paths were systematically expanded and made suitable for horses and oxen. With the construction of the first roads over the Gotthard, the stagecoach era finally began in 1830 – however, this ground to a halt in 1882 when the Gotthard Railway began operating through the new tunnel. In the early 20th century, the first motorists appeared on the pass, and the road underwent further improvements. With the boom in individual transport and mass tourism in the post-war era, the Gotthard Road was developed into its current form. By 1980, the first road tunnel through the Gotthard massif shortened the once arduous, multi-day journey through the Alps to a 15-minute drive.

Therefore, on the saddle of a bicycle, a motorbike or at the wheel of a car, travellers can experience the Gotthard as one giant open-air museum – a more than 800-year-old cultural structure, whose trails once clung precariously to the Alpine topography and whose route over the centuries has become increasingly closer to the ideal of the fastest and shortest connection, as the crow flies. We may marvel at the Devil's Bridge and the zigzag of the Tremola, thinking nostalgically of the old days when traversing a pass was still an experience. But historically, even the most beautiful bridges and delightful serpentines have always had just one purpose: to shorten the travel time between the north and south, to make the trip faster, safer and more comfortable.

It seems more than a little ironic that we, the ones who have come so close to maximum acceleration, now haunt the old routes on racing bikes and in hard-suspension sports cars with the express desire to deliberately prolong the once-feared journey over the Gotthard. The old Uri folk would have most likely shaken their heads in disbelief. Yet, we postmodern people have long known, of course, that with every evolutionary step in mobility, a piece of human experience

hen und die einst so gefürchtete Fahrt über den Gotthard als Erlebnis der Entschleunigung zu zelebrieren. Die alten Urner, so ist zu vermuten, hätten wohl verständnislos den Kopf geschüttelt.

Doch wir postmodernen Wesen wissen natürlich längst, dass mit jeder Evolutionsstufe der Mobilität auch ein Stück menschlicher Erfahrung verloren gegangen ist, das man sich nun mühevoll wieder beschaffen muss. Es ist dieses neuzeitliche Bedürfnis nach echten, ungefilterten Erlebnissen, welches uns das Steuer eines klassischen Porsche 356 Speedster aus den 1950er-Jahren ergreifen lässt – der mit seinem spartanischen Verdeck ja nicht viel mehr ist als ein Zwei-Mann-Zelt auf Rädern. Es ist der Wunsch nach Motorenlärm, Benzingeruch und dem Gefühl, über Lenkrad, Schaltung, Gas und Bremse

is lost, which now must be painstakingly recaptured. It is this modern-day yearning for real, unfiltered experiences, which allows us to take the wheel of a classic Porsche 356 Speedster from the 1950s, which, with its minimalistic top, is basically not much more than a two-man tent on wheels. It is the desire for the roar of an engine, the smell of petrol, and the feeling of the road through the steering wheel, gearshift, throttle and brakes, which makes us climb behind the wheel of historic racing cars such as the Porsche 911 Carrera RS, or even a Porsche 906, and tackle the Alpine passes.

In fact, a vintage sports car is the ideal medium to admire the architecture of the Tremola and the other masterfully built sections of the Gotthard not only from afar, but indeed to experience this with all the senses:

direkt mit der Straße in Verbindung zu stehen, die uns in einen historischen Rennwagen wie den Porsche 911 Carrera RS – oder sogar einen Porsche 906 – steigen und die Passhöhen der Alpen erklimmen lässt.

Tatsächlich ist ein alter Sportwagen das ideale Interface, um die Architektur der Tremola und all der anderen meisterhaft konstruierten Streckenabschnitte am Gotthard nicht nur aus der Entfernung bewundernd zu betrachten, sondern die Steigung, die Kurvenradien, die Beschaffenheit der Pflastersteine auch tatsächlich am ganzen Körper zu erspüren und zu erfahren. Am Steuer dieser leichten, puristischen und aglien Maschinen bekommt man zudem ein Gespür dafür, was es selbst vor 50 Jahren noch bedeutete, über den Gotthard nach Süden zu reisen: Der Aufstieg durch die wilde Schöllenenschlucht, die plötzliche Weite der Landschaft des Urserentals, die heimliche Freude am Pass angesichts der armen Zeitgenossen, die keinen »Luftgekühlten« besitzen und mit offenen Hauben warten müssen, bis ihr Kühlwasser wieder auf Betriebstemperatur heruntergekühlt ist, die ersten Indizien für das nahende Italien in den Tälern des Tessins. Steigt man aus dem einfachen Klassiker in einen modernen Porsche 911 oder gar ein Hybrid-Wunderwerk wie den Porsche 918 Spyder, verbindet sich mit einem Schlag der Traum vom authentischen Erlebnis der Passüberquerung mit dem hyperbeschleunigten Komfort der Tunnelfahrt. Man gleitet so sanft und hermetisch von der Außenwelt abgeschirmt über den Pass, als säße man im Kino, lässt sich von Thom Yorke in Dolby Surround den epischen Soundtrack einspielen – und gebietet mit einem leichten Druck auf die Pedalerie über gewaltige Beschleunigungs- und Verzögerungskräfte, die jederzeit entfesselt werden können.

Natürlich spürt man die Fliehkräfte in den engen Kehren des Gotthards stärker als auf den schnurgeraden Autobahnen im Tal – doch das eigentliche Erlebnis der Passfahrt liegt nicht im stumpfen Ausreizen der Grenzen der Physik, sondern im freudvollen »Lesen« der Landschaft mithilfe einer Fahrmaschine, die ausschließlich zu diesem Zweck geschaffen scheint. Und wer die Geschichte der Gotthardstraße kennt, der braucht seiner Vorstellungskraft nur einen kleinen Schubs zu geben, und schon kann er sie vor sich sehen: Die alten Säumer auf ihrem beschwerlichen Marsch durch die Schöllenenschlucht. Die gelbe Postkutsche bei vollem Galopp in den Kurven der Tremola. Die schwarzen Dampfloks in den Kehrtunnels über Wassen. Die ersten Automobilisten im Schatten ihrer eignen Staubfahnen. Die schweren Militärlastwagen auf ihrer Fahrt ins Réduit. Die Touristenbusse der Nachkriegszeit auf dem Weg nach Italien.

Einst werden auch wir mit unseren zeitgenössischen Sportwagen, Motorrädern und Velos nicht mehr sein als unscharfe Erinnerungen, als nostalgische Bilder aus einer längst vergangenen Zeit – und ein weiteres Kapitel in der ewigen Gotthard-Geschichte.

to feel the ascent, the sweeping hairpins, the texture of the cobblestones, with the whole body. At the wheel of these lightweight, minimalistic and nimble machines, one also gets a sense of how it must have felt even 50 years ago to travel south across the Gotthard: the climb through the wild Schöllenen Gorge, the sudden expanse of the Urner Valley landscape, the quiet smugness as our 'poor' contemporaries in their 'non-air-cooled' cars stand at the top with the hood open waiting for the radiator fluid to cool. And finally, the first signs of Italy as we wind our way down into the valleys of Ticino.

Switching from the simple classic into a modern Porsche 911 or even a hybrid miracle such as the Porsche 918 Spyder, and the dream of the authentic experience of traversing the pass goes from slow-mo to hyper-accelerated comfort. Gliding over the pass so smoothly and hermetically sealed from the outside world, as if sitting in a cinema, accompanied by the epic soundtrack of Thom Yorke in Dolby Surround Sound – unleashing, at will, tremendous acceleration and deceleration forces with the slight twitch of a pedal.

Of course, you feel the g-force in the tight switchbacks of the Gotthard more than on the dead straight autobahns in the valleys, however, the real experience of the pass is not in the dull thrashing of the limits of physics, but rather in the delightful 'reading' of the landscape with the help of a driving machine that seems to have been created precisely for this purpose.

And those who already know the history of the Gotthard Road need only give their imaginations a little nudge, and they can immediately see before their eyes the old-timers on their gruelling trek through the Schöllenen Gorge; the yellow stagecoach of the Swiss Post at full gallop through the curves of the Tremola; the black steam locomotive chugging through the spiral tunnels above Wassen; the first motorists in the shadows of their own dust trails; the thundering military convoys on their way to the Redoubt; and the tourist buses of the post-war era on the way to Italy.

One day, we too with our contemporary sports cars, motorbikes and bicycles will be just hazy memories, nostalgic images from a by-gone era – just another chapter in the long and illustrious story of the Gotthard.

GOTTHARD · PORSCHE DRIVE

DRIVE — 337

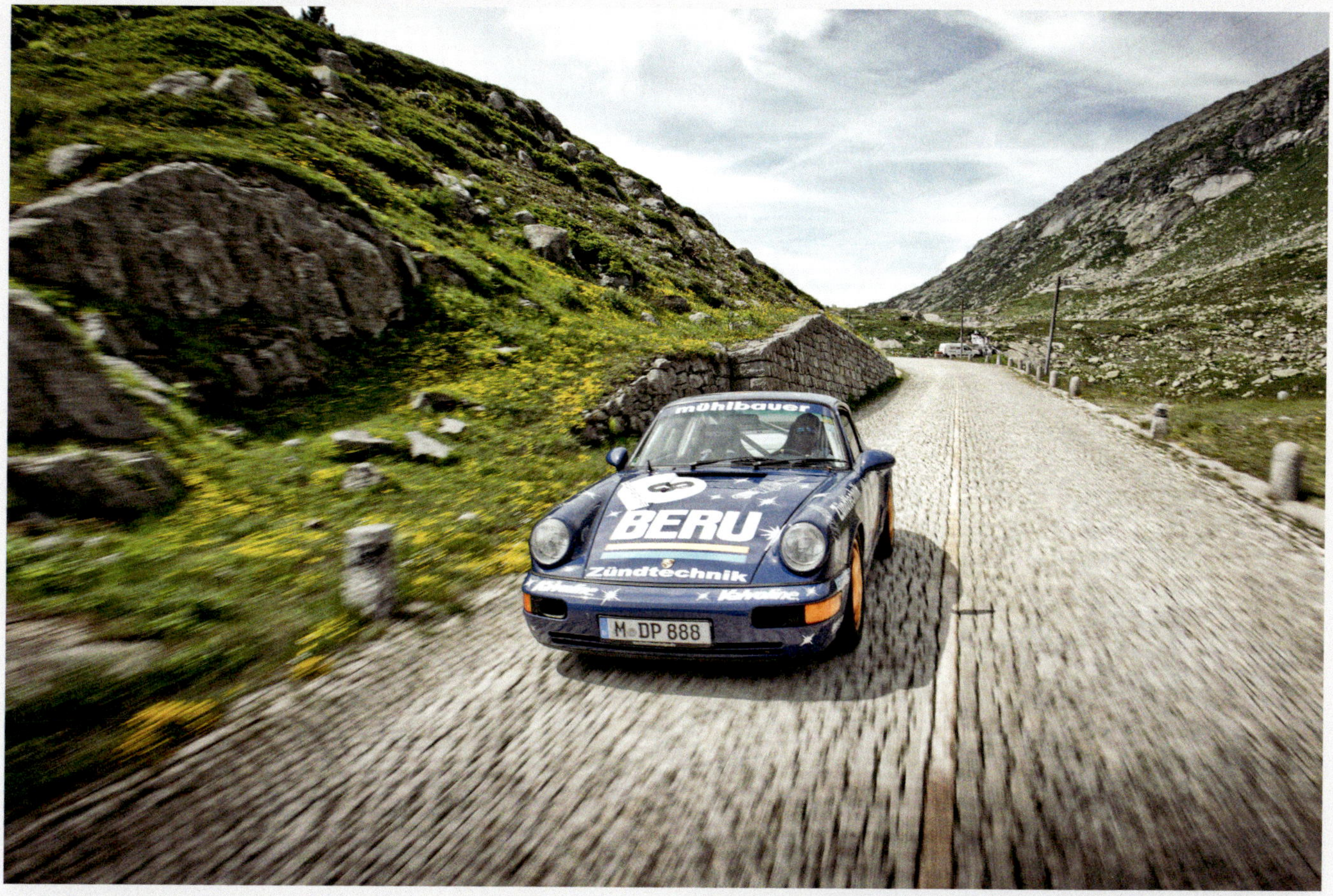
mühlbauer
BERU
Zündtechnik
M DP 888

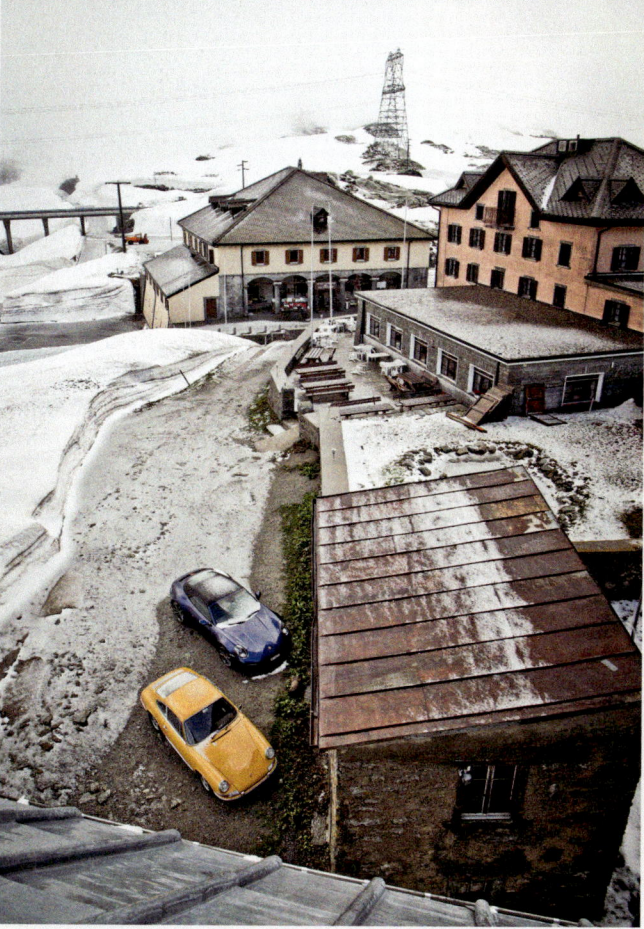

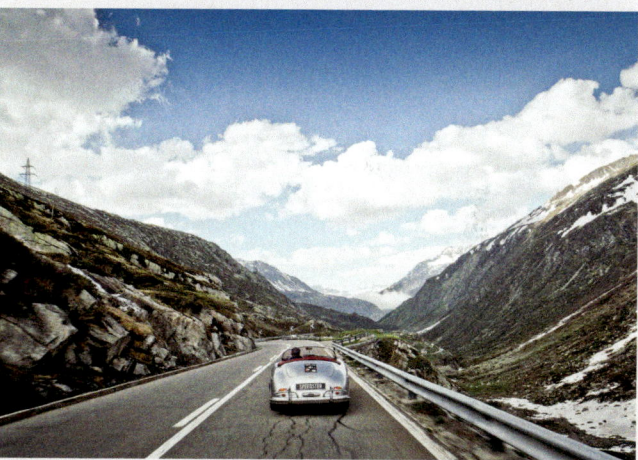

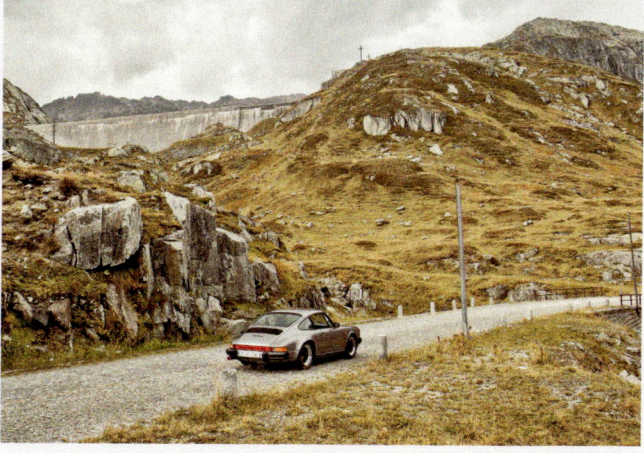

354 — DRIVE PORSCHE DRIVE · GOTTHARD

GOTTHARD · PORSCHE DRIVE · DRIVE — 355

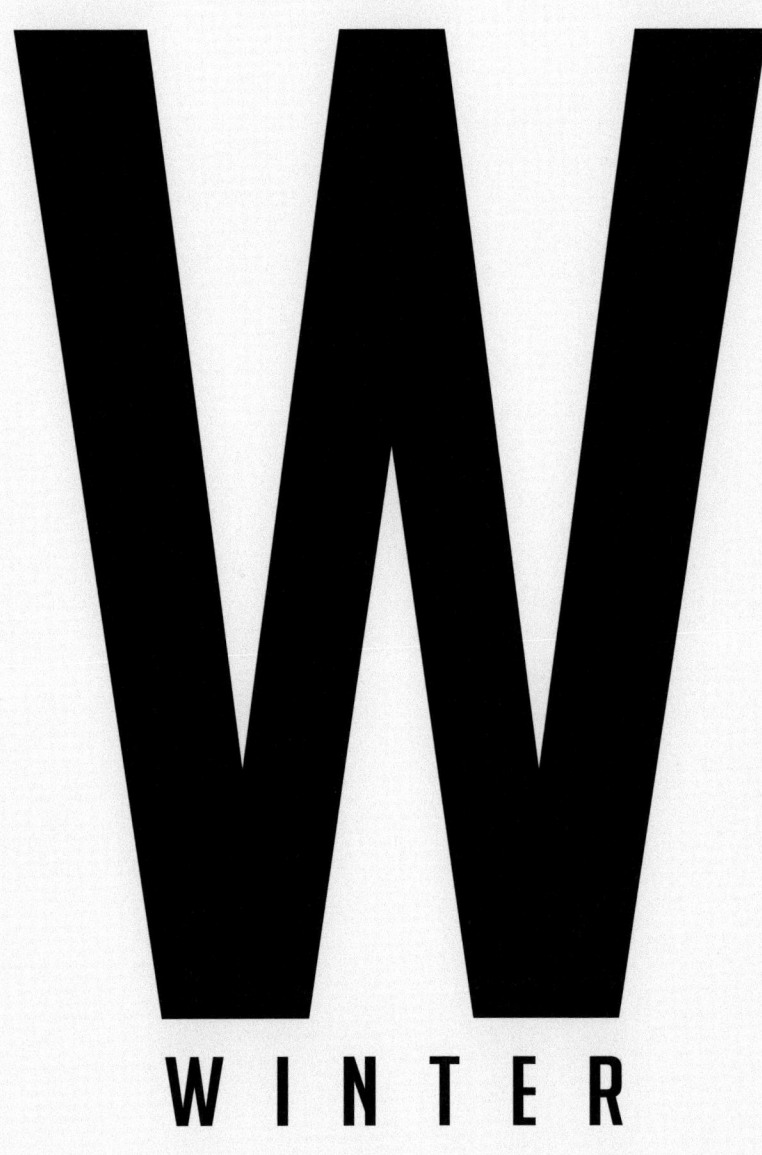

REISETIPPS / TRAVEL TIPS

– ESSEN, TRINKEN, ÜBERNACHTEN

Hotel & Restaurant Gotthard, Gurtnellen In der nostalgischen Gaststube des Restaurant Gotthard in Gurtnellen ist die Zeit stehen geblieben – und das ist wirklich gut so! Mit Silberbesteck löffelt man Kraftbrühe, zerlegt die frisch gebratene Bachforelle oder macht sich über die Zitronencreme à la mode her. Nach dieser formidablen Stärkung könnte man den Gotthard eigentlich auch zu Fuß überqueren.

Hotel Sonne, Andermatt Nostalgisches Gasthaus im Herzen von Andermatt mit uriger Stube, herzhafter schweizerischer Küche, freundlichem Personal und einfachen, aber gemütlichen Zimmern. Im Haus gegenüber hat 1799 General Suworow gewohnt. Uns dient die »Sonne« auf unseren Reisen zum Gotthard-, Furka-, Grimsel- und Sustenpass stets als Basislager.

Hotel Bären, Andermatt Im Hotel Bären in Andermatt findet man moderne Zimmer mit alpinem Twist; der eigentliche Grund für einen Besuch ist jedoch das von Gault & Millau empfohlene Restaurant, das neben verfeinerten Klassikern der Tessiner Küche je nach Saison auch Wildsau und Murmeltier auf den Tisch bringt.

– EAT, DRINK & SLEEP

Hotel & Restaurant Gotthard, Gurtnellen Time has stood still in the nostalgic dining room of the Restaurant Gotthard in Gurtnellen – and that's perfect! With silver cutlery, one can spoon out the clear broth, slice up the freshly baked brown trout or devour the Zitronencreme à la mode. Duly fortified, one is almost tempted to cross the Gotthard on foot.

Hotel Sonne, Andermatt Hotel Sonne is a nostalgic guest house in the heart of Andermatt with a rustic parlour, hearty Swiss cuisine, friendly staff and simple yet cosy rooms. In 1799, General Suvorov lived in the house across the street. The 'Sun' served as the base camp for our travels to the Gotthard, Furka, Grimsel and Susten Passes.

Hotel Bären, Andermatt Hotel Bären in Andermatt offers modern rooms with an Alpine twist; however, the real reason for a visit is the restaurant recommended by Gault & Millau, which serves refined Ticino classics and, depending on the season, wild boar and marmot.

Hotel St. Gotthard, Hospental The Baroque house of the Hotel St. Gotthard in Hospental dates back to the year 1722 and

Hotel St. Gotthard, Hospental Das Barockhaus des Hotel St. Gotthard in Hospental stammt aus dem Jahr 1722 – und entsprechend gemütlich geht es im Restaurant des Hauses zu. Beim Blick in die Karte hat man die Wahl zwischen Lammleber mit Butterrösti oder Saltimbocca mit Safranrisotto. Und wer nach reichhaltigem Mahl nicht mehr weiterreisen möchte, dem empfehlen wir das historische Gästezimmer, in dem man so herrlich nostalgisch nächtigen kann wie zur Zeit der Gotthardpostkutschen.

Vecchio Ospizio San Gottardo Das Alte Hospiz an der Gotthard-Passhöhe ist sicherlich die ästhetisch anspruchsvollste Unterkunft an der Passstraße. Einst fanden hier Pilger und Händler auf ihrem beschwerlichen Weg über den Gotthard Zuflucht vor Wind und Wetter, heute zieht das Hotel – dank einer kunstvollen Modernisierung durch das Basler Architekturbüro Miller & Maranta – vor allem Designliebhaber an. Eine Nacht in den minimalistischen, nach Fichtenholz duftenden Zimmern vergisst man sein ganzes Leben lang nicht.

Restaurants an der Passhöhe Wer an der Gotthard-Passhöhe einkehren möchte, hat die Wahl zwischen dem Restaurant Prosa, dem Restaurant Alte Sust und der Militärküche, wo man die kulinarischen Klassiker der Schweizer Armee wie Käseschnitten, Hörnli mit Hackfleisch, Schüblig mit Kartoffelsalat und Wurstsalat mit Käse verkosten kann. Wer keine Zeit verlieren möchte, dem sei am Pass eine Kalbsbratwurst oder Cervelat vom Grill oder ein Stück Tessiner Käse vom Spezialitätenstand aus Airolo empfohlen.

La Claustra In einem alten Bunker des Gotthard-Reduits findet sich seit dem Jahr 2004 das exzentrische Felsenhotel La Claustra. Die »Oase im Berg« verfügt über 17 individuell gestaltete und klimatisierte Zimmer, abends wird ein Sechs-Gang-Menü mit regionalen Spezialitäten serviert. Wer am Gotthard in Klausur gehen möchte, ist hier richtig.

Bike & Breakfast Airolo / Osteria Tremola Mit dem Bike & Breakfast finden Rennradfahrer in Airolo am Fuße des Gotthardpasses nicht nur ein neues, einladendes Basislager – in der Osteria Tremola wird auch noch Erstklassiges aufgetischt. Chefkoch Luca Brughelli kombiniert regionale und saisonale Produkte wie Felchen und Lamm zu einem kreativen Geschmacksfeuerwerk, das gekonnt zwischen traditioneller und molekularer Küche schwingt.

Locanda Orelli Die Locanda Orelli im Bedrettotal liegt zwar nicht an der Gotthard-Passstraße – doch wer unserer Empfehlung für eine »große Passrundfahrt« in Richtung Nufenenpass folgt, sollte bei Alessandro Manfrè Station machen. Auf den Tisch kommen interessante Variationen der Tessiner Bergküche wie Ravioli mit Eselfleisch oder Risotto mit Bärlauchpesto.

the hotel restaurant is equally as authentic. The menu offers delicacies like lamb's liver with butter rösti or Saltimbocca on a saffron risotto. For those who wish to stay after such a sumptuous feast, we recommend enjoying a nostalgic night in one of the historic guest rooms reminiscent of the Gotthard mail coach era.

Vecchio Ospizio San Gottardo The Altes Hospiz at the Gotthard Pass summit is definitely the most aesthetically appealing accommodation on the pass road. Pilgrims and traders once took refuge here from the wild wind and weather on their arduous journey over the Gotthard. Thanks to its new contemporary look by the Basel-based architectural firm Miller & Maranta, the hotel now attracts many visitors, particularly lovers of design. A night in the minimalistic spruce-scented room is certain to remain a lifelong memory.

Restaurants at the Top of the Pass Stop off for a bite to eat at the top of the pass: visitors have a choice between Restaurant Prosa, Restaurant Alte Sust and the Military Kitchen for authentic Swiss Army culinary classics such as fondues, pasta with mince, smoked sausage with potato salad, wurst salad and cheese. For those in a hurry, we suggest grabbing a veal bratwurst or Cervelat from the grill or a wedge of Ticino cheese from the Airolo speciality stand.

La Claustra An old bunker of the Gotthard Redoubt now houses the eccentric Felsenhotel La Claustra. This 'mountain oasis' boasts 17 individually designed, air-conditioned rooms, with guests served a six-course dinner featuring regional specialties. Staying here is a real Gotthard treat.

Bike & Breakfast Airolo / Osteria Tremola At Bike & Breakfast, racing cyclists not only find a new and inviting base camp in Airolo at the foot of the Gotthard Pass, they also enjoy first-class cuisine in the Osteria Tremola. Chef Luca Brughelli combines regional and seasonal products, such as whitefish and lamb, to create a tastebud sensation that skilfully swings between traditional and molecular cuisine.

Locanda Orelli The Locanda Orelli in the Bedretto Valley is not actually on the Gotthard Pass Road, however if you follow our recommendation to take the 'great mountain pass' towards the Nufenen Pass, it is definitely worth stopping at Alessandro Manfrè's establishment. Here, they serve interesting variations of Ticino mountain cuisine such as ravioli filled with donkey meat or risotto with wild garlic pesto.

— UNTERNEHMEN UND ENTDECKEN

Nationales Gotthardmuseum In der »Alten Sust« an der Passhöhe hat die Stifung Pro San Gottardo das Nationale St. Gotthard-Museum eingerichtet, in dem die mehr als 800-jährige Geschichte des Alpenpasses anhand von Originaldokumenten, Kunstwerken und Objekten nacherzählt wird. Mit etwas Glück trifft man nebenan im Restaurant den Museumsdirektor Carlo Peterposten, der Neugierigen wirklich jedes Detail zur Geschichte des Gotthards erläutern kann.

Sasso San Gottardo Unweit der Passhöhe befindet sich der Eingang zur unterirdischen Erlebniswelt des »Sasso San Gottardo«. In den 1940er-Jahren als militärische Festungsanlage und Teil des »Réduit national« gebaut, sind die Geschützräume, Munitionsmagazine, Massenunterkünfte und kilometerlangen Tunnels heute Teil eines Museums der ganz besonderen Art. Neben den gut erhaltenen Artefakten der historischen Festungsanlage »Sasso da Pigna« kann man im »Sasso San Gottardo« auch interessante Wechselausstellungen, Kunstinstallationen und eine eindrucksvolle Sammlung gewaltiger Bergkristalle bestaunen.

Historisches Museum Uri Die Geschichte des Kantons Uri und der Gründungsepos der Eidgenossenschaft ist fest verwoben mit der Historie des Gotthardpasses. Im Historischen Museum Uri in Altdorf kann man die Besiedlungsgeschichte des Urnerlandes von den ersten steinzeitlichen Menschen über das Mittelalter bis in die Moderne erleben. Der Verkehrsgeschichte ist dabei ein eigener Raum gewidmet.

Historische Zugfahrten Die 1882 eröffnete Gotthardbahn mit ihren Kehrtunnels und Galerien ist eine der spektakulärsten Eisenbahnstrecken der Schweiz. Seit der Eröffnung des Basistunnels im Jahr 2016 besitzt die alte Zugstrecke zwar keine verkehrspolitische Relevanz mehr – die SBB organisiert auf der Gotthardstrecke jedoch immer wieder touristische Fahrten mit alten Dampfloks und legendären elektrischen Alpenlokomotiven wie der »Krokodil«.

Postkutschenfahrten Wer wissen möchte, wie sich eine Reise über die Alpen zur Zeit der Postkutschen vor 150 Jahren anfühlte, kann eine Fahrt im historischen Landau Coupé der Gotthardpost buchen. Der Fünfspänner mit Postillon und Konducteur startet in Andermatt und fährt über die Passhöhe und die alte Tremolastraße hinab nach Airolo.

Wanderwege Die Passstraße über den Gotthard ist vor allem für Automobilisten, Rad- und Motorradfahrer interessant. Doch man kann das Massiv auch wunderbar zu Fuß erkunden – etwa auf dem Vier-Quellen-Weg zu den Ursprungsorten von Rhein, Reuss, Tessin und Rhone oder auf den Spuren der Säumer auf dem Gotthard-Wanderweg.

— ADVENTURE AND DISCOVERY

National Gotthard Museum In the 'Alten Sust' at the top of the pass, the Pro San Gottardo Foundation has established the National St. Gotthard Museum, which retraces the 800-year-old story of the Alpine Pass with original documents, works of art and objects. With a little luck, you will meet the museum director Carlo Peterposten, who is happy to explain the detailed history of the Gotthard to curious visitors.

Sasso San Gottardo Not far from the pass summit is the entrance to the underground world of the 'Sasso San Gottardo'. Built in the 1940s as a military fortress as part of the Swiss National Redoubt, the cannon chambers, ammunition magazines, dormitory-style accommodation and kilometres of tunnels are now part of a very unusual museum. Aside from the well-preserved artefacts of the historic 'Sasso da Pigna' fortress, visitors can also marvel at the interesting temporary exhibitions, art installations and an impressive collection of massive mountain crystals.

Uri Historical Museum The story of the Canton of Uri and Switzerland's foundation is tightly interwoven into the history of the Gotthard Pass. In the Uri Historical Museum at Altdorf one can experience the colonisation history of the Urnerland from the first Stone Age people through to the Middle Ages and modern times. The history of traffic needs its own separate room.

Historic Train Rides The Gotthard Railway, which opened in 1882, with its spiral tunnels and galleries, is one of the most spectacular railway lines in Switzerland. Since the establishment of a base tunnel in 2016, the old train track is no longer used for transporting goods, however the SBB organises tourist trips on the Gotthard line with old steam trains and legendary electric Alpine locomotives like the 'Crocodile'.

Stagecoach Rides Those who are curious to find out what a journey across the Alps felt like 150 years ago should book a trip in the historic Landau Coupé of the Gotthard Post. The five-horse coach with postilion and conductor starts at Andermatt and heads over the pass and descends over the old Tremola Road to Airolo.

Hiking Trails The pass road over the Gotthard is particularly interesting for motorists, cyclists and motorbike riders. However, the massif can be explored on foot, for example the Vier Quellen Weg (Four Springs Trail) leads to the sources of the four rivers Rhine, Reuss, Ticino and Rhone or follows in the footsteps of the muleteers on the Gottardo Hiking Trail.

VIELEN DANK/THANK YOU:

Wir möchten uns herzlich bedanken bei: Kaya Demiroglu und Ralph Aschwanden von der Bildungs- und Kulturdirektion des Kantons Uri, Urs Oberholzer von der Baudirektion des Kantons Uri und Gianmarco Talamona von der Repubblica e Cantone Ticino, die uns wertvolle Einblicke in die historischen Dokumente rund um den Bau der Gotthardstraße gewährt haben. Dem Schneeräumungsteam aus dem Kanton Tessin, das uns die Tremolastraße für Fotoaufnahmen geöffnet hat. Marzio Eusebio, dem Hotelier des Ospizio San Gottardo, für die Gastfreundschaft und die spannenden Passgeschichten. Carlo Peterposten, der uns durch das Gotthard-Museum am Pass geführt und viele Fragen beantwortet hat. Damian Zingg und den Mitarbeitern aus dem Sasso San Gottardo für die interessanten Einblicke ins Bunkerleben. Linda Russi von der Andermatt-Urserntal Tourismus GmbH für die wertvollen Tipps und Kontakte. Den Piloten von SwissHelicopter für die Perspektivwechsel. Martin Brandenburg, Roland Richter, David zu Elfe, Phil und dem Team von DJI für die eindrucksvollen Film und Drohnenaufnahmen. Michael Dorn, der den Bildern und dem Buch den letzten Schliff gibt. Philipp Hohenthanner for being the »Instacharlie«. Und natürlich allen Sportfahrern, die uns trotz Regen, Sturm und Schnee immer wieder auf den Gotthard begleitet haben: Marco Marinello, Nikolas Knoll, P&P Patt, Franz Schwarz, Max von Braunmühl, Tobias Aichele, Hermann Köpf, Malte Fromm, Bernd Georgi und Michael Daiminger. Ein großer Dank für die Unterstützung unserer Produktionen gilt auch Porsche, Porsche Deutschland und dem Porsche Museum. Und natürlich Nadja Kneissler, Birgit Radebold, Jörn Heese, Kaye Mueller, Eva Grieger und Axel Gerber vom Delius Klasing Verlag für das Vertrauen und die Unterstützung.

We would like to sincerely thank: Kaya Demiroglu and Ralph Aschwanden from the Department of Education and Culture for the Uri canton, Urs Oberholzer from the Uri canton Building Department and Gianmarco Talamona from the Repubblica e Cantone Ticino, who gave invaluable insights into the historic documents on the building of the Gotthard Road. The snow-clearing team from the canton of Ticino, who opened the Tremola Road for a photo shoot. Marzio Eusebio, the hotelier of the Ospizio San Gottardo, for the warm hospitality and gripping stories about the pass. Carlo Peterposten, who showed us through the Gotthard Museum at the pass and answered many questions. Damian Zingg and the staff at the Sasso San Gottardo for the fascinating glimpses of bunker life. Linda Russi from Andermatt-Urserntal Tourismus GmbH for the helpful tips and contacts. The pilots from SwissHelicopter for a new perspective. Martin Brandenburg, Roland Richter, David zu Elfe, Phil and the team at DJI for the impressive film and drone footage. Michael Dorn, who added the final touch to the images and the book. Philipp Hohenthanner for being the »Instacharlie«. And, of course, all the drivers who accompanied us on the Gotthard through rain, storm and snow: Marco Marinello, Nikolas Knoll, P&P Patt, Franz Schwarz, Max von Braunmühl, Tobias Aichele, Hermann Köpf, Malte Fromm, Bernd Georgi and Michael Daiminger. A huge thank you to Porsche, Porsche Deutschland and the Porsche Museum for helping with the production. And, last but definitely not least, thank you to Nadja Kneissler, Birgit Radebold, Jörn Heese, Kaye Mueller, Eva Grieger and Axel Gerber from Delius Klasing Verlag for your confidence and assistance.

Stefan Bogner

Für Micha, Maxi & Dominik, die die Kurven im Alltag driften. Den Kurvenverstehern bei Porsche, die uns immer unkompliziert unter die Arme greifen. Und Jan Karl, ohne dich als Sparringspartner würde es diese wunderbaren Projekte nicht geben. Vollgas forever!

For Micha, Maxi & Dominik, who negotiate the zigzags of everyday life. The cornering allies at Porsche for their unfailing and uncomplicated assistance. And Jan Karl. Without you as my sparring partner, these wonderful projects would never exist. Full throttle forever!

Jan Karl Baedeker

Für Laura, Anton und Luise – meine liebsten Reisebegleiter. Mein herzlicher Dank gilt: Laura für die mentale und logistische Unterstützung meiner Buchprojekte – ohne Dich wäre das Blatt noch leer. Meiner Mutter Elke Baedeker und meiner Großmutter Gertrud Hadwich für die vielen schönen und inspirierenden Reisen über den Gotthard nach Süden, die in mir die Freude am Reisen und Entdecken geweckt haben. Weiterhin möchte ich mich bedanken bei Dr. Christine Lesmeister und Inga Konen von Porsche Schweiz für den passenden Reisewagen für meine Recherchen. Dem Literaturhaus Zürich für viel Raum zum Schreiben, Inspiration, Kaffee und einen wunderbaren Alpenblick. Und natürlich auch meinem lieben „Kurvenspezi" Stefan Bogner, der mich zum Berg gebracht hat und weiterhin unermüdlich durch die Serpentinen scheucht. Die Reise geht weiter.

For Laura, Anton and Luise – my favourite travel companions. My heartfelt thanks to Laura for supporting me with my book projects psychologically and logistically – without you these pages would be empty. My mother Elke Baedeker and my grandmother Gertrud Hadwich for the many wonderful and inspiring trips over the Gotthard to the south, which awakened in me a joy of travel and discovery. Moreover, I'd like to thank Dr Christine Lesmeister and Inga Konen from Porsche Switzerland for providing the perfect car for my research. The Literaturhaus Zürich for the room to write, inspiration, coffee and the spectacular Alpine view. And, of course, to my dear 'cornering buddy' Stefan Bogner, who got me through the mountain serpentines safely and unflaggingly. The journey continues.

Bibliografische Information der Deutschen Nationalbibliothek
Die Deutsche Nationalbibliothek verzeichnet diese Publikation in der Deutschen Nationalbibliografie; detaillierte bibliografische Daten sind im Internet über http://dnb.dnb.de abrufbar.

Bibliographic information published by the Deutsche Nationalbibliothek. The Deutsche Nationalbibliothek lists this publication in the Deutsche Nationalbibliografie; detailed bibliographic data are available in the Internet at http://dnb.dnb.de.

1. Auflage / 1st edition
ISBN 978-3-667-11677-2
© Delius Klasing & Co. KG, Bielefeld

Konzept/Concept: Stefan Bogner
Einbandgestaltung und Layout/Cover Design and Layout: Stefan Bogner
Text: Jan Karl Baedeker
Übersetzung ins Englische/Translation: Kaye Mueller
Fotos/Photos: Stefan Bogner
Motivausarbeitung/Artwork: Michael Dorn

Projektmanagement und Lektorat/
Projectmanagement and Editor: Birgit Radebold
Produktion/Production: Jörn Heese, Axel Gerber
Druck/Printing: Firmengruppe APPL, aprinta-druck, Wemding.
Printed in Germany 2019

Alle Rechte vorbehalten! Ohne ausdrückliche Erlaubnis des Verlages darf das Werk weder komplett noch teilweise reproduziert, übertragen oder kopiert werden, wie z. B. manuell oder mithilfe elektronischer und mechanischer Systeme inklusive Fotokopieren, Bandaufzeichnung und Datenspeicherung.

All rights reserved. The work may neither be entirely nor partially reproduced, transmitted or copied – such as manually or by means of electronic and mechanical systems, including photo-copying, tape recording and data storage – without explicit permission of the publisher.

Delius Klasing Verlag, Siekerwall 21,
D - 33602 Bielefeld, Germany
Telefon/Phone +49 (0)521 559-0,
Telefax/Fax +49 (0)521 559-115
E-Mail: info@delius-klasing.de
www.delius-klasing.de

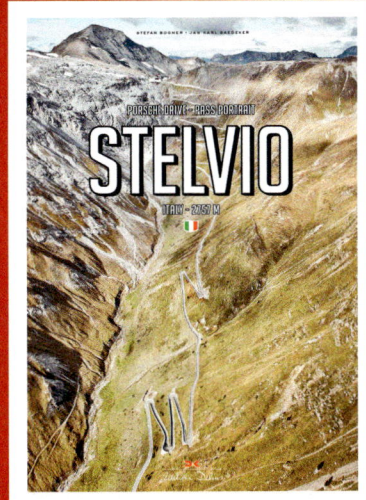

»STELVIO«
DAS STILFSER JOCH

»GROSSGLOCKNER«
DIE GROSSGLOCKNER
HOCHALPENSTRASSE

PYRENÄEN
PYRENEES
Im Handel erhältlich/Available in stores

ÖSTERREICH
AUSTRIA
Im Handel erhältlich/Available in stores

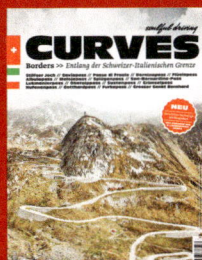

SCHWEIZ
SWITZERLAND
Im Handel erhältlich/Available in stores

SCHOTTLAND
SCOTLAND
Im Handel erhältlich/Available in stores

FRANKREICH
FRANCE
Im Handel erhältlich/Available in stores

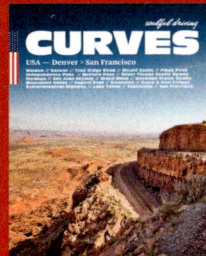

USA • COLORADO
USA • COLORADO
Im Handel erhältlich/Available in stores

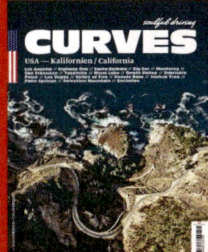

USA • KALIFORNIEN
USA • CALIFORNIA
Im Handel erhältlich/Available in stores

SIZILIEN
SICILY
Im Handel erhältlich/Available in stores

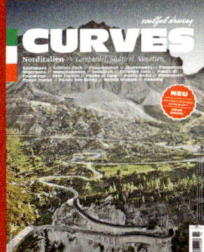

NORDITALIEN
NORTHERN ITALY
Im Handel erhältlich/Available in stores

DEUTSCHLAND/DÄNE.
GERMANY/DENMARK
Im Handel erhältlich/Available in stores

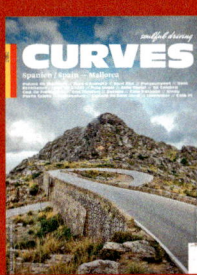

SPANIEN MALLORCA
SPAIN MALLORCA
Im Handel erhältlich/Available in stores

ESCAPES
TRAUMROUTEN DER ALPEN
IM HANDEL ERHÄLTLICH

TRACKS
NÜRBURGRING NORDSCHLEIFE
IM HANDEL ERHÄLTLICH

PORSCHE DRIVE
15 PÄSSE IN 4 TAGEN
IM HANDEL ERHÄLTLICH

CARS AND CURVES
A TRIBUTE TO
70 YEARS OF PORSCHE
IM HANDEL ERHÄLTLICH